Lessons on Mastering M
Some reflections...

"What Fred really offers here is a roadmap that any young person can follow to the financial freedom they'll crave in their later years."

Mike Farwell
TV & Radio Talk Show Host, Broadcasting - Radio & Television, Conestoga College
and BA – English, University of Waterloo

"Where was this book when I was 21? Mr. Masters' book hits the mark when it comes to instantly increasing the level of financial literacy for Canada's young people; it will improve their financial future and set them on a path to financial freedom."

Laura Shoemaker
Superintendent of Learning (retired), OCT, EdD, University of Toronto

"I learned about personal finance by reading David Chilton's book, *The Wealthy Barber*; for today's young Canadians, it will be *Lessons on Mastering Money*. I know I will be giving *Lessons on Mastering Money* to my two daughters; it will provide any young Canadian with the needed foundation for a successful personal financial journey!"

Chris Woodcroft
Superintendent of Student Achievement, Secondary, OCT
MEd, Wilfrid Laurier University and Two-time Canadian Olympian (Wrestling)

"*Lessons on Mastering Money* hits the mark when it comes to helping younger Canadians understand and successfully navigate a financial world that can be overwhelming. It can certainly be said that *Lessons on Mastering Money* delivers the critical foundational lessons that are absolutely necessary for a successful financial life!"

Colin R. Westman
Judge (retired), Ontario Court of Justice (1990 – 2018)

"I would expect the reader to finish this book feeling excited, informed and hopeful about financial challenges that lay ahead."

J. Stephen Schmidt
LL.B., Juris Doctor, University of Toronto

"The resource is aimed at our youth but also serves as a refresher course for all who are concerned about managing their own money. His advice is practical, easy to follow, clear and understandable."

Roger Lawler
Director of Education (retired), MA, Carleton University and MEd, University of Toronto

1

"*Lessons on Mastering Money* provides comprehensive information that is critical for building a solid foundation to help achieve success in all key areas of a person's financial life."

John Collings
CPA, CA, CISA, CIA, Director - Internal Audit (retired)

"Whatever your current financial situation may be, *Lessons on Mastering Money* is sure to offer critical strategies that will immediately improve your overall financial well-being."

Jacob Robinson
Investment Analyst and former VP-Finance of DECA Laurier
BBA, Wilfrid Laurier University

"Navigating personal finances always seemed frightening, but after reading this book I feel that I have armed myself with the necessary tools to navigate my own finances."

Andrew Pickett
Professional Athlete (Football), BSc, University of Guelph

"No matter where you're at on your personal finance journey, *Lessons on Mastering Money* will help you take better control of your financial life!"

Jenna Weishar
People and Culture Specialist, BA – Psychology and Sociology, Wilfrid Laurier University and Graduate Certificate, Human Resources Management, Conestoga College

"I highly recommend this guide for anyone, especially students or new graduates who have the ability to develop good saving habits right from the start! "

Karolina Deoniziak
Innovation Manager, BBA, Wilfrid Laurier University

"*Lessons on Mastering Money* is the perfect book at the perfect time for young Canadians!"

Robel J. Berhane
Executive Coordinator, BCom, Entrepreneurship, St. Mary's University

"This book contains what we should have all been taught in school about money!"

Jack Quirke
Software Product Manager, BBA, Wilfrid Laurier University

"I would recommend this book to my fellow high school and university students as well as recent graduates, as it provides the guidance we need to set ourselves up for financial success, and live the lifestyles we desire."

Hunter Tyszka
BBA, BA – Financial Mathematics Double Degree Student, Wilfrid Laurier University

Lessons
on
Mastering
Money

The Personal Finance Guide for
Canadians in their 20s & 30s

~Delivered by an experienced finance teacher~

Fred J. Masters, BBA, BEd, PQP
President & Founder, Masters Money Management

Printed in Canada

ISBN 978-1-7778920-0-5

FIN 10 11 2021

Disclaimer:

This work contains the author's opinions and ideas as related to the subject matter. The content is by no means designed to provide any reader with individual financial advice. Note that past performance is not a guarantee of future results when it comes to any specific investment or investment strategy. Always consult a competent financial professional for advice when it comes to making financial decisions. No guarantee is made with respect to the accuracy or completeness of the content, especially given the changes that occur in this subject field over time. Nothing in this work constitutes advice and no one connected with its creation is responsible for any use of the information contained therein or for any action taken or representation made based on its contents. The author, publisher and/or any of their respective agents, successors, assigns, employees, shareholders, associates, servants, insurers, subsidiaries, and/or related companies, assume no liability for any damages whatsoever including, without limitation, indirect, special, consequential, punitive or incidental damages of any kind, whether brought in contract, tort, or negligence, whatsoever arising in any way and relating to any act, transaction, occurrence or event, connected with, or arising out of the use, reliance upon, or performance of any material contained in book, even if expressly advised of the possibility of such damages.

Editor: Daina Feick

Dedication

This book is dedicated to YOU! It's dedicated to YOU because:

- I know that you desperately want to increase your level of financial literacy NOW;

- I know how difficult it is to thrive financially without this knowledge NOW;

- I know that money worries are a huge source of stress for you NOW;

- And I know that you never learned any personal finance in school but you will NOW!

I see that you have been added to my class list. I'm so happy you're here!

I can help. Let's get started!

Mr. Masters

The author would like to extend sincere appreciation to the following experts who graciously performed peer review work as noted below. Your rich feedback was deeply valued!

Michael Hincks, PhD (Part I – Mastering the Money Mindset)

Angelika Jarski, CPA, CA (Part II – Mastering Debt)

Curtis Shea, CPA, CA (Part III – Mastering Investing)

Mason Leite, CFP, RRC (Part IV – Mastering Your RRSP, RESP & TFSA)

Emil Sabo, AST, CALE (Part V – Mastering Your Ride)

Richard Ventura, BBA, PFP, AMP (Part VI – Mastering Real Estate)

The author would like to recognize the work of Daina Feick, who professionally edited this book.

Contents

Foreword

Lessons on Mastering Money is a brilliant book that will be a 'game-changer' when it comes to helping Canada's young people significantly increase their level of personal financial awareness. It provides impressively thorough and meaningful insights on an essential life skill that we all want to master!

Leveraging his decades of experience teaching financial literacy, Mr. Masters has written an incredibly comprehensive yet accessible guide that will allow any young Canadian to thrive financially. Written with empathy and using a conversational style, this book should be mandatory reading for any graduate who is ready to enter the workforce. Implementing the advice found here will put any reader on the path to achieving their financial goals. It should be viewed as the foundational guide for understanding the world of personal finance for Canada's young people.

This is the finest personal finance book that I have ever read.

David Kohler
FP Canada™ Fellow
Professor of Financial Planning Services, Conestoga College
BBA, Wilfrid Laurier University, MBA, McMaster University
CLU, CHFC, CFP

Preamble

My name is Fred Masters. I am a retired teacher. I am also the President & Founder of Masters Money Management and a licensed mortgage agent. I have an absolute passion for teaching others about personal finance. As a matter of fact, I have been doing it since the '80s. This passion has led me to this moment, and I am excited to share my story and my lessons with you!

I graduated from Wilfrid Laurier University's School of Business & Economics (now known as the Lazaridis School of Business & Economics) with an Honours Bachelor of Business Administration degree. During my years at Laurier, I was able to gain a significant amount of business-related work experience through summer jobs and the co-operative education program. I worked for one of the Big Four accounting firms, a global consumer products company, a major Canadian financial institution and for a marketing firm that was tasked with launching a province-wide campaign for a well-known agricultural organization. I loved finance and was well on my way to a career in business.

My girlfriend, who is now my wife (Kathy Doherty-Masters), was heavily involved in coaching ringette as a young adult. I decided to get my coaching certification and join her on the bench as a coach. I came to realize that I absolutely loved to coach; I got a natural high from it.

I loved finance. I loved to coach. How could I do both? I could teach finance.

With this clarity in mind, I applied to Western University's Faculty of Education and graduated from teachers' college with senior qualifications in accounting. I applied for one school board, had one interview and was hired full-time by the Waterloo Catholic District School Board (WCDSB) based out of Waterloo Region, located in southern Ontario.

Over the next twenty-nine years, I loved what I did! I taught for one year at Monsignor Doyle Catholic Secondary School in Cambridge, ON and transferred to Resurrection Catholic Secondary School in Kitchener, ON when it opened. I stayed at 'Rez' for the rest of my career except for one year when I took on a system-wide consultancy role for the school board. In total, I spent half of my career in positions of added responsibility, including board-level Experiential Learning, Careers & Technological Education Consultant and school-level Program Head of Business & Co-operative Education. I taught senior finance and co-operative education virtually every semester over my entire career.

I completed both parts of the principal qualification program (PQP) but I made the decision to not pursue a principalship. In doing so, I 'left lots of money on the table'. My rationale? I loved teaching, and becoming a principal would mean that I couldn't do that anymore. The PQP experience was certainly beneficial but the discernment process that I undertook led me to stay in the classroom.

In hindsight, this was definitely the right call.

Towards the latter part of my career, I noticed that my senior students were 'feeling it' when it came to money. They were working huge hours – some worked as many as 35 hours a week at 'part-time' jobs – and they were under immense pressure to save. They knew what was coming – tuition and housing costs for post-secondary programs are big – and when I would ask why they were working so many hours, they invariably would tell me that they needed to come up with money for school. Sometimes they were the second or third child heading to university or college and there was just no family money left, or sometimes their parents had told them straight up that they wouldn't be receiving any family financial help for school costs. Those kids were pushing on all levels. Many succumbed to the pressures and didn't manage to get the marks they wanted to gain admission offers to their first post-secondary program of choice. Those part-time jobs proved to be very expensive in many ways.

I knew I could help them. I decided to start a club. I called it Phoenix Finance (Resurrection's school teams are called Phoenix) and I would run a weekly 'lunch and learn' session. I would open up a classroom, welcome whomever wanted to drop in, encourage them to bring their lunch and teach them personal financial literacy.

It was a risky undertaking at best.

I had no idea whether any kids would want to give up one of their lunch periods each week to listen to some teacher lecture about a topic when they wouldn't even earn a credit for attending.

The kids did indeed show up. During the last five years of my career, I put on over 100 sessions. Some students attended every year from grade 9 right through to grade 12. Staff members started attending too. Word about the club spread quickly and I was asked to do an interview by a local TV station and create a workshop presentation for the WCDSB's Wellness Committee.

Then, one of those moments happened: during the fall of Phoenix Finance's second year, Andriy Shkilko, an Associate Professor of Finance at Wilfrid Laurier University, reached out regarding the club. He ended up coming out to see a session. Of particular note is that Professor Shkilko also held the position of 'Canada Research Chair in Financial Markets' at the time. It became very clear that I could take Phoenix Finance (and my passion for teaching others about personal finance) with me into retirement and launch a business.

I retired early – two days after my 53rd birthday – and launched Masters Money Management during my last month of teaching. At the same time, some of my former students and co-operative education employers with whom I worked reached out with job offers. The fall after I retired, I became a licensed mortgage agent with Mortgage InGenuity Inc. out of Kitchener. The lead broker is one of my former students. He still calls me Mr. Masters – love it!

I have now made dozens and dozens of personal financial literacy presentations, both in person and virtually, since Masters Money Management launched in 2018. I have presented to university students – Wilfrid Laurier University contracted with me to put on nine virtual financial literacy sessions for their students during the 2020-2021 academic year – and also to both secondary and elementary students. School boards have partnered with me to put on board-wide presentations for parents and staff members. I have presented to employees of both not-for-profit organizations and businesses.

I have learned that there is an insatiable appetite to learn more about personal finance, especially amongst our young adults. Those in their 20s and 30s are often overwhelmed financially. It's not their fault – many have been taught virtually nothing at all about the topic of personal finance. My experiences as a licensed mortgage agent have certainly confirmed this.

Media outlets - The Globe and Mail, Waterloo Region's newspaper (The Record), CBC Radio One KW, NewsTalk1010 out of Toronto and Kitchener's CityNews 570 – have all reached out with interview requests in regards to financial literacy in the schools.

My goals during all my presentations and media appearances are simple. I want to help others increase their level of personal financial literacy. I want to help others better understand money. I want to help others feel empowered when it comes to making personal financial decisions. I want to help others successfully navigate life's personal financial journey.

I want to continue my life's work: teaching others about money.

Is it working? From my teaching days, I know the importance of a feedback loop so after each of my presentations and media appearances, I collect feedback. My business site – www.mastersmoneymanagement.ca – is full of these testimonials. Here are a few of my favourites:

"I look forward to every conversation with Fred because I always come away with another nugget to add to my own financial planning. His passion for keeping our spending in check and his matter-of-fact approach that's easy to understand make Fred the perfect guest to deliver timeless and relevant information to my audience. Smart, sound, and savvy advice. I wish I'd met Fred 40 years ago!"

Mike Farwell, TV & Radio Talk Show Host

"Dejero was looking for someone to help the overall financial literacy of employees. Fred delivered on exactly what we were looking for through 'Your Money 201', bringing zeal and enthusiasm to a not so excitable topic. Fred left our team wanting more - looking forward to having him in for 'Your Money 301' in the near future!"

Jenna Weishar, People and Culture Specialist, Dejero

"Animated, compelling, sobering and dynamic! I didn't want it to end! Fred Masters' Money 101 session was excellent! Fred clearly knows his subject matter and he knows how to deliver financial guidance in a relevant and effective way to a diverse audience. I highly recommend his expert advice to the young and those no so young."

Dean Sherk, Development Officer, Wilfrid Laurier University

I love making these presentations and the feedback has encouraged me to continue on this pathway. After being quoted in The Globe and Mail for the first time, I was contacted by an individual who shares my passion for teaching personal finance. That individual connected me with Professor Fred Selinger, who is a leading personal finance author in the United States and a lecturer at the Haas School of Business at the University of California at Berkeley. Those conversations led to my decision to write this book.

My presentations have helped attendees become more confident financially.

A book, though, filled with lessons from my presentations, could help so many more people face financial challenges with confidence. To that extent, financially empowering Canadians – specifically those in their 20s and 30s – was the objective as I wrote this book.

Introduction

Money, in and of itself, won't make you happy. But not having enough money – or constantly worrying about money – is a major stressor. Are Canadians feeling anxious when it comes to their personal finances? Survey after survey sadly indicates that this is definitely the reality for many. Money worries are the number one source of stress for surveyed Canadians – ranking ahead of work, relationships or even health. Half of Canadians surveyed say that financial stress has caused them to lose sleep. For those under the age of 35, a whopping eighty-five per cent indicate that they have at least one financial regret and almost sixty per cent state that financial worries have impacted their life in at least one way.[1] For those surveyed Canadians who are feeling financial stress, over half state that they are worried about their ability to retire.[2] Clearly, this deep, deep sense of financial anxiety is like a debilitating wave that is washing across the entire country.

During my teaching days, I would ask my students to go home and pose this question to Mom during dinner time when Dad and the family were there: "Mom, how much could you spend without checking with Dad first?" You should have heard the stories that they brought back to the next class! As Canadians, we just don't talk about money – it's seen as a taboo subject, like sex and religion. Some affluent families do talk about money since they know how important it is to have a high level of financial literacy in order to make good financial decisions.

Don't blame yourself if you feel you don't know much about money; you've got lots of company. Personal finance rarely appears in required courses in this country, nor in other countries. In Denmark, three-quarters of young adults state that they have little or no knowledge about interest rates. Meanwhile, in the United States, only one-quarter of young adults know about inflation, and can perform simple interest calculations.[3] You can even study commerce or business administration at a prestigious Canadian university and graduate without learning any mandatory personal finance content during your four years. You will learn lots of finance at a business school, but it will be 'financial accounting' or 'taxation' or even 'auditing'. It likely won't be personal finance.

Why is this the case? A recent survey indicates that Canadian kids really want to learn about money. The topics they want to learn about aren't surprising – how to manage money, how to save money, how to choose a career that will help earn money and how to invest. The survey also indicates that our kids state that they are not learning these money basics in school nor at home.[4]

The Organisation for Economic Co-operation and Development (OECD) declared that "Poor financial decisions can have a long-lasting impact on individuals, their families and society."[5] It stated that "Financial education can make a difference. It can empower and equip young people with the knowledge, skills and confidence to take charge of their lives and build a more secure future for themselves and their families."[6] The OECD also noted that "Low levels of financial literacy have also been associated with a lower standard of living, decreased psychological and physical well-being and greater reliance on government support."[7]

Why, then, don't our kids learn much, much more financial literacy in schools?

We are in the midst of a personal financial crisis in this country from coast to coast to coast. The Bank of Canada has been sounding the warning alarm for years that Canadians are taking on way more debt than they can afford. Many are suffering in silence since we just don't talk about money, and we certainly don't teach about it.

The goal of this book is to empower you – Canadian adults in their 20s and 30s – with the core personal financial literacy knowledge needed to control your money on your life's personal financial journey.

No one should care about your financial well-being more than you. Delegating your financial decision making to another person, such as a family member or an advisor, leaves you financially blind. You need to be able to ask the right questions and stay involved in the conversations; you need to be at the table so as to understand the decisions. Success in any organization can often be traced back to strong leadership. Surely, you have witnessed this in your life in countless settings. Once you view your financial life as a very, very important business, then you will instantly recognize that you must put steps in place to financially prosper. Look in the mirror – the person staring back at you owns your financial success. By the way, 'hoping' for the best financial outcome isn't going to cut it; you need to understand the financial game because you play it every day of your adult life, and this is one game that we can all win!

There are many personal financial hurdles to overcome in life. Three of the biggest financial tests are saving enough for retirement, saving for the kids' education and solving the housing-affordability puzzle successfully. These three are crucial. You MUST pass all three of these major financial tests or you will struggle mightily with your financial life – getting just one right or even two of the three right is just not good enough. You need to get 100% right on this test, and this book provides help with all three of these pieces. Saying that Canadians struggle with debt is a total understatement; there's help here for this too. A recurring mistake that many Canadians make financially is leasing a brand-new car – there's guidance around this also. Getting a handle on how you think about and approach your personal finances – your money mindset – is really bedrock learning; all good financial decisions lead right back to this. The book begins by teaching you these key money mindset lessons.

The format of the book aligns with the biggest personal financial hurdles that Canadians face. It is broken down into six major thematic sections:

i) Mastering the Money Mindset

ii) Mastering Debt

iii) Mastering Investing

iv) Mastering Your RRSP, RESP & TFSA

v) Mastering Your Ride

vi) Mastering Real Estate

Each section is full of practical, tangible, understandable lessons designed to help any Canadian – but especially those in their 20s and 30s – take control of their financial life in these crucial areas.

The book is written in a similar style to my Masters Money Management personal financial literacy presentations. It is full of foundational, core personal finance lessons. The language is clear and understandable. The content is mostly practical with a wee bit of theory in some places to make the backdrop (which is usually the economy) a bit easier to grasp. Although the target is Canadians who are in their 20s and 30s, those older and younger can certainly apply many of the practical personal finance tips that are found throughout the book.

Even if you have delegated control over your financial affairs to someone else, such as a family member or an advisor, you absolutely must understand what's going on with your money. This is a non-negotiable. This book's content will allow you to be way more confident when it comes to being involved in those financial decisions. You'll understand what's happening. You'll feel empowered when it comes to making personal financial decisions.

Guiding you...financially! That about sums up the purpose of the book! No one should care about your money more than you.

You're going to meet Penny. Penny is the face of Masters Money Management. She is the cute little green piggybank that appears on the book's cover. She also appears throughout the book. When you see Penny make an appearance, pay special attention because that lesson is a foundational, core one! Penny will have something to say about it in her pithy way. Action these tips – your future self with thank you for it!

The advice is simple but not easy to follow; you will understand the lessons, but implementing them during your life's personal financial journey will be a challenge. You've got this – and Penny is here to help!

Part I

Mastering the
Money Mindset

In 'Mastering the Money Mindset', we'll discuss a wide variety of foundational personal finance lessons that are absolutely crucial to understand. When approaching a major challenge, it's always important to have the proper mindset before beginning. This is absolutely true when it comes to your financial life – your 'money mindset' matters. Your money mindset is the set of money-related values and beliefs that drive your life's personal financial decisions. Actioning the key money mindset lessons found here will put you in position to take the necessary steps to enjoy financial success. This is the starting point for taking control of your financial life.

Crucial lessons in this part of the book include the importance of embracing gratitude, being a saver as opposed to a spender, being involved in financial decision making and managing your financial expectations.

The foundation for an empowering money mindset is outlined here.

Embrace an 'attitude of gratitude'!

Mastering the 'money mindset' requires a multi-faceted approach to positively shaping your outlook on your personal finances. It involves way more than one thing. Having said that, it must start with this first lesson – embrace an 'attitude of gratitude' – since attitude is really everything!

Be intentional about being thankful for all that you have on every level. Be mindful about it; spend time reflecting on it daily. Let it permeate who you are. Those who are thankful and appreciate what they have are happy. Those who are unhappy are constantly focusing on what's missing in their lives. This unhappiness can lead to rampant spending financed via cheap debt.

What does this look like? It can take the form of six figure balances on lines of credit to finance spending on vehicles when large raises never materialized, or it can be second mortgages on the family home to consolidate tens of thousands of dollars of credit card spending on stuff.

The first step to getting control of your money is to embrace an 'attitude of gratitude'. Make a list – mentally or write it down – of three things for which you are thankful at the end of every night. Shift away from thinking about what's missing in your life and focus instead on being thankful. Learn to deeply appreciate the many wonderful pieces and individuals in your life and express that to others! Show it through words and action; share your good fortune and many gifts. Pay it forward! Nurturing an 'attitude of gratitude' is one of the keys to lifelong happiness.

Penny says...

Recognize that an 'attitude of gratitude' is the foundation to a healthy relationship with money and a key part of having a positive 'money mindset'! If you have a life partner, it's a collective effort since you both need to be on the same page in order to experience success with this key aspect of your journey together.

Collect memories – not stuff!

Think of your best memory from last year or the year before that. It will likely be time spent with others experiencing fun things together that might have sentimental value, such as enjoying a special meal together to celebrate an occasion, or a family vacation or taking in an event that you really enjoyed. It won't be buying stuff! Be intentional about choosing experiences over stuff! Spend money on experiences as opposed to stuff. Gift experiences as opposed to buying more stuff. Spending time together creates memories – and those memories are priceless!

This can be a family initiative when it comes to gift giving. Instead of shopping for stuff, give one another a shared experience, such as a family pass to see a movie, or a family trip to a favourite festival, event or game, or whatever resonates with your family. Once you are intentional about this approach, the benefits will become crystal clear. Remember, focus on less stuff and instead embrace shared experiences! Time together is priceless whereas stuff becomes clutter.

Be a minimalist. Being a minimalist doesn't mean you lead a boring, bland life. It means that you don't collect stuff which will clutter your life. It will lead you to 'mindful' spending which beats 'mindless' spending. Collect memories instead of stuff! Spend time enjoying experiences with those close to you.

Do you really need a new winter coat? If you need it, want it and can afford it, get it. Take the time, though, to pull out the winter coat that just became obsolete, thank it for its service and donate it. Often, we just collect, collect, collect stuff. If you go for a walk in many suburban neighbourhoods in this country and you look inside people's garages, they are so jammed with stuff that fewer and fewer people park cars in their garages anymore. Avoid that trap. You will spend less and avoid the personal stress that comes from drowning in clutter.

Make good financial decisions daily – and repeat

Putting yourself in a position to thrive financially requires self-control. You need to make good 'micro' or small financial decisions throughout the day today – and then do the same tomorrow. Deferred gratification is the goal. Instead of dropping by your local coffee shop twice daily with your partner to grab your favourite $7 lattes, make something at home and take the drinks with you. That simple decision alone can translate to over $10,000 a year in savings and could fund two outstanding family vacations.

Penny says...

Making good financial decisions each day is wise.
Your future self will thank you!

The 'earn, save, invest cycle'

This is foundational. You must earn income before you can start to save money, and you must save money in order to be in a position to invest. You must get these three pieces all right and put plans in place to repeat this cycle again and again over the long term to prosper financially. This will put you in a position to achieve financial milestones, such as funding your children's post-secondary costs (if applicable), retiring with financial freedom and controlling your levels of debt. Think of this cycle as the teacher's solution set for controlling your financial life!

Penny says...

Earn, save, invest...and prosper! There is no other way to effectively take control of your money. 'Winning the lottery' just cannot be your long-term financial plan!

Just 'earning' isn't enough – finding work you love is the goal!

Yes, 'earning' involves finding a job and earning money. Recognize, however, that work is often pure drudgery for many, many people. You are going to work tens of thousands of hours over your lifetime. Work can be 'just a job' but we all want it to be much more than that. Align your education and experiences with a sector you love and you will increase your chances of finding work that gives you joy. When you are passionate about your work, the years float by gently like a summer breeze. Not crazy about your current job? Love it or plan to leave it!

This involves a journey inside first. What do I love? What are my passions? Can I pursue my passions as work?

Talk to your mentors. Don't have a mentor? Get one – or more! They may be around you already! Consider those who you respect and who know you well, such as family members, colleagues at work, your teachers/instructors, coaches and other connections.

Plan your career path and keep your eyes open for roles that you would like. Align your own additional educational choices with what's needed to secure your dream job. Invest in yourself! You rarely are truly ever 'done school'. Subsequent degrees, certifications, and experiences all help you to stretch and grow! This is a key way to position yourself to secure meaningful, satisfying work and also puts you in position to grow your income over time. This is a crucial piece since income dollars fund savings, and savings is used for investing, and investing helps us to reach our major financial goals. If income stagnates, our goals become harder to reach.

Still finding your way? Be intentional about your educational pathway since this is often the best indicator of your earning potential. Going to university simply because your friends are going is not the right reason. A

26

little-known fact is that many university students either change their programs on the way to graduation or don't graduate at all. This is both expensive and demoralizing; it can be a huge hit to your self-esteem. Take steps to avoid this!

Penny says...

Be a lifelong learner – be curious and have an appetite to keep learning. You will grow and prosper, and the work will not feel like work. You will become an expert in your field and, over the years, that should lead to increased earning potential given your growing expertise and experience.

Employment advice for now and also for the kids when the time comes - hello 'separators'!

If you have kids, encourage them to explore, explore, explore as they grow up. This will broaden their perspective and give them a better chance to find what they love.

Exploring can happen in many ways. It can mean taking a variety of elective courses during high school years. It can mean volunteering. It can mean getting involved in extracurricular activities that present leadership opportunities. Make no mistake – 'grit' and 'resiliency' are often learned in these extracurricular settings. Acquiring these skills prepares young people for the challenges that every adult repeatedly faces in life.

Encourage the kids to actively seek out experiential learning opportunities. Co-operative education programs and internships at the high school and post-secondary level offer outstanding opportunities to 'test drive' a field. When completed during high school, this can lead to making better, more informed decisions about post-secondary pathways. When done at the post-secondary level, co-operative education placements are usually paid, which is a plus. However, the benefits here go well beyond the money. University or college co-operative education placements open the door to gaining fantastic sector-specific work experience. These learning experiences often open the door to securing that coveted job. Volunteering also offers many of the same benefits and rewards, despite the low pay!

These experiences all allow students to gain access to mentors who can be a wonderful source of wisdom during pivotal years.

They also offer opportunities for students to accumulate what I call 'separators' which are unique experiences that bring with them 'in demand' transferable skills that position people to 'get that first dream job' or 'grab that promotion'. Separators are those pieces of one's story that 'separate' them from the crowd and give them a competitive advantage. For a student-athlete who participates in a team sport, it's their wealth of teamwork experience and learned grit. For someone who has accumulated significant volunteer experience, it's the predisposition to give of one's self. These are separators. Yes, you need to have technical expertise that is taught in a given college or university program. I would often tell my senior finance students that they were going to graduate from their university or college program – with hundreds of others! However, those who get the best employment offers have the separators. Be sure to encourage your kids to not only collect their 'separators' but also capture them on every employment application, resume and cover letter that they prepare!

All of these pieces are found on the path to finding work that gives you joy. Those who seek out separators are giving themselves an advantage when it comes to finding dream jobs!

You have a choice; you are either a saver or a spender – time to decide!

This sounds obvious but you have to save more than you spend. Live within your means. Get a handle on your spending to see if your dollars are going towards goods and services you want versus what you need. Have a strong self-awareness level regarding your own spending habits. Remember that shopping isn't a form of therapy, nor is it a recreational activity.

How are we doing with this absolute core tenant of personal finance? Let's consider a few survey results. Over forty per cent of surveyed Canadians don't think that they can cover their living expenses without taking on more debt. The same percentage are concerned about their debt level. Only about thirty per cent feel that they would be able to cope with unexpected bills without taking on more debt. Only about half of those surveyed under 35 years of age felt that their bank account could handle another financial emergency.[1]

When we think about saving for retirement, the picture is equally bleak. Three out of ten Canadians surveyed have no retirement savings – none. Millennials believe that they'll need to head into retirement with over $900,000 saved, but 90% of Canadians admit they don't even have a retirement plan in place. On average, Canadians say they've only saved about $180,000 for retirement so far.[2]

Those results aren't very encouraging.

Don't think about saving – 'autosave'!

Clearly, budgeting and setting financial goals are very challenging for many people. Here's an alternative. 'Autosave' large, large chunks of your income after every payday arrives, and move the money to a separate bank account at a virtual bank so that it's inconvenient to access the cash. Save until it hurts. It should be a struggle to live on what you keep in your main operating bank account. This will allow you to save a significant percentage of your take home pay. Have extra cash left in your account when the next payday arrives? You didn't save enough; increase your savings rate going forward.

If you are in a relationship, you MUST have both partners on-board here. This is a non-negotiable.

Once your savings arrive in your virtual bank, auto divide the dollars into different accounts or 'buckets' by savings goal and label them as such. You know the needs since they never seem to go away: emergency fund, vacation, car repair, new car, house repair, retirement, kids' schooling costs, kids' activity costs, first or next home, etc.

Live in the world of 'likely' when it comes to identifying these future costs. Are you *likely* to want to go on vacation next summer? Are you *likely* going to need to do some house repairs soon? Are you *likely* going to have to spend some money on car repairs in the coming months? If it's likely, start saving for it! To be honest, major costs are all 'likely' coming; they're real and large. Yes, you will be disappointed to learn that your car needs an unexpected $1,000 repair, but your future self will thank you because you have the money saved to pay that bill.

Importantly, the beauty of the autosave system is that you are both budgeting and saving to support reaching your financial goals without even knowing it. Think about that for a moment. By diverting money after each payday to savings buckets, you budget and set financial goals and action those goals through the autosave system.

Deferred gratification will put you on the road to taking control of your money. That's the formula for saving – we'll cover investing a bit later.

Penny says...

The autosave system is an absolute key financial lesson to learn. It's simple to understand but difficult to action. Commit to this strategy to reach your financial goals. As Ben Franklin once said, "By failing to prepare, you prepare to fail." See it a different way – by succeeding at planning, you are planning on succeeding! Penny loves it!

Beware of FOMO – it can sabotage your savings program!

FOMO – fear of missing out – is a powerful force in our financial lives. Over half of millennials feel pressure to keep up with their friends' and colleagues' financial status.[3]

Social media does all kinds of damage here. We see others post their fantastic experiences and wonder, "What's wrong with me?" as we scroll through posts. What you don't see is that some of those posts are made by people who have tens of thousands of dollars of crushing credit card debt from previous vacations or who are still paying off car debts from vehicles that they got rid of years ago.

Make no effort to keep up with your neighbours' spending habits. Focus on your savings program and embrace being a minimalist. Yes, you see your neighbours' 'big ticket' purchases since they are often parked in the driveway; what you don't see is a listing of their debts.

Set spending limits and stick to them!

This is especially true when it comes to gift giving but it can also apply on a biweekly basis. Are you prone to making impulse buys? Then consider giving yourself an 'allowance' to cover each two-week pay period and, when the money is gone, it's gone. This will sharpen your awareness around your spending habits and help you to take control of your money. This is also a great exercise for couples who struggle to make ends meet at the end of each pay period.

When it comes time to holiday, vacation and birthday spending, set a limit that you can live with so as to avoid the shock that comes with opening up a credit card bill after a spending binge. You know these costs are coming; you can even list them out. The solution? Save for them each payday! It's so much better to approach an expensive time of the year knowing that you have the cash tucked away to pay for the upcoming costs, as opposed to having to carry a balance on your credit card or dip into the line of credit to pay for a vacation. Blue Monday falls in January for a reason, and it's not just because of the weather; a big part of it is the post-holiday credit card bill shock!

Penny says...

'Setting spending limits' is really the basis of budgeting. The money that comes into your account each payday isn't all 'fun money'. Much of it will, in fact, go towards costs that come around each month. You can monitor and track these costs. Getting a handle on your budget is a very wise financial exercise for anyone who is serious about taking control of their money!

The most important decision (both financial and non-financial) of your life is your life partner – choose very wisely!

Money is often cited as a top cause of divorce, and having partners on different pages with respect to money is a recipe for disaster.[4] Divorce is tough – very tough – on many levels, and this includes being a financial challenge.

Want to take a positive step towards regaining control of your financial life? Strengthen your relationship with your life partner!

Remember that your life partner's debts will become your debts too. You must, therefore, have many courageous conversations about money – and spending patterns – with your partner well before the relationship becomes too serious. Make these conversations regularly scheduled events. Put these meetings – they could be weekly or monthly but at least quarterly – in your phone, and make time to talk about money so that you are continually both pulling on the same financial rope. The alternative is a road filled with financial challenges. There's a reason why speed dating clubs often require members to bring their credit scores on 'date nights'!

Penny says...

Talk to your honey about money! Just like anything else, handling money is much easier if you are both committed to it, do it together and support one another through the challenges! Remember, there's nothing sexier than a good credit score!

Loyalty matters - be a relationship builder in all facets of your life!

When you are a service provider and have a client that is a repeat customer over many years, you are appreciative of that client's loyalty. This is important since it builds trust, and that trust goes both ways. You should know your automotive mechanic's name, and they should know you, too. It's important to have strong business relationships in all parts of your life that you build on over the years. Be intentional about having long-term business relationships with your mechanic, plumber, electrician, lawyer, financial advisor, insurance agent, family doctor and dentist, to name just a few.

Be sure to provide referrals to others for these service providers also; that goes a long way to strengthening those business relationships. Need to access a new service provider? Ask your connections for a referral so that you are in a position to leverage your existing network.

By the way, continually working on your personal relationships is one of the core tenants for a happy life, so be certain that this is an absolute top-of-mind priority on a daily basis!

Realize, though, that all businesses need customers and 'ask' accordingly

Being loyal certainly doesn't mean that you need to be 'blindly loyal'. It's much easier and cheaper for any business to keep existing clients than to find new ones. This opens the door for you to do what many do not do – ASK for discounts when it makes sense. For example, check out promotions that other service providers are offering on cell phone, internet and TV bundles, and call your service provider to see if they can price match. Always ask to be transferred to the 'loyalty department' to get to a customer service representative who has discretion around pricing. Those representatives are tasked with keeping clients (keeping the churn rate low), and they will take steps to keep your business. These service providers often offer special promotional pricing, so consider switching providers to lock in better pricing. The monthly savings can quickly add up to hundreds of extra dollars annually.

Don't be afraid to follow this approach in many other areas too. Notice that your bank assessed a large service charge last month because your balance dipped below a certain threshold unexpectedly? Call customer support and request that it be rolled back. You can't do this continually but, again, businesses want to keep your business, so 'ask' accordingly!

Be strategic with your points – and take the cash when you can!

'Cash is king' so take cash rewards as opposed to point rewards whenever possible. Collecting points at a retailer that you rarely frequent is ideal for the retailer because you may change your spending habits in their favour – but it's wrong for you. Start with this question – 'Do I shop here or buy these products on a regular basis?' If the answer is 'yes', then by all means consider joining their loyalty program! This also works when you are considering incurring an ongoing membership fee to obtain the right to shop in a store! If the savings on items that you need easily tops the cost of the annual membership fee, then the membership makes sense.

Layer points when possible. Using a cash back credit card to book a hotel stay where you collect points is a delightful 'double dip'!

Be absolutely certain that there's value in a rewards program or a credit card before paying any type of annual fee.

Use an industry-wide loyalty points provider if it allows you to collect points and earn rewards in a sector where you frequently spend money, as opposed to a particular chain's points program. This allows you the flexibility to find good deals but doesn't restrict you to using a particular chain or retailer. Spending more while booking a stay with a given hotel chain just to hit some points threshold is not a strategy that benefits you in the long run.

Government emergency benefits don't last forever – don't ever view them as your financial safety net!

Take responsibility for creating your own financial safety net so that you never find yourself in a position where you need to be bailed out by any government.

The COVID-19 pandemic brought with it a horrible death toll, as hundreds of thousands of people around the globe lost their lives. It also brought economic destruction. Governments moved quickly to push out emergency relief monies to citizens who experienced sudden job losses as a result of pandemic-related shutdowns. These monies led to government deficits soaring to unprecedented levels.

The economic supports were needed to avoid a deep depression. However, there will be consequences for all that spending. Government bailouts don't last forever, and citizens will pay the price.

Most people don't want their taxes to go up. Most people don't want to pay more for government services. It does seem inevitable, though, that taxes will go up for some. Strong stock market performance certainly opens the door to increasing taxes connected to capital gains on investments. Strong housing market performance certainly open the door to increasing property taxes. It also seems inevitable that the cost for government services – from ice rental fees to toll road charges – will rise. None of these measures will be popular.

Yes, we have seen short-term government emergency financial stimulus monies flow out when a huge financial shock hits. However, food still has to be bought and rent or the mortgage still needs to be paid, along with all of the other costs that come with living in this day and age. Never count on governments to bail you out financially.

You need an emergency fund...for emergencies!

You may have heard the phrase 'emergency fund' before and thought that those emergencies will pass you by. You'll dodge those economic bullets, right? We should perhaps rename it a 'shock & awe fund'. Why? When a financial emergency comes, it will be like a shot to your financial gut. Having a financial safety net – available cash – isn't going to diminish the 'shock'. It is, however, going to provide you with a path forward so that you have a way to get by the 'awe'.

Make no mistake, financial storms are coming. Unexpected bills will be arriving – not 'if', but 'when'. They will never arrive 'at a good time'; they will always arrive 'at the worst possible time'. An unexpected pay cut or job loss are also examples of a financial shock, as is a broadly felt crisis like the global pandemic. You will never be happy to see these financial shocks arrive. However, if you have an emergency fund in place, at least you will know that you have the money to get through the storm. You will not be thrown into financial despair.

Having an emergency fund is an absolute non-negotiable. Yet, sadly, 20% of Canadians stated that they could not come up with $2,000 on short notice to cover off an emergency expense.[5] This is just asking 'financial stress' to come sit at the kitchen table and stay for awhile.

An emergency fund will also allow you to leave a job that you don't enjoy so as to search for a job that's a better fit; the emergency fund will buy you time to do the hunting.

One of my Masters Money Management presentation attendees called me many months after the pandemic started. She had attended an in-person session with her three kids – ages 16, 18 and 22 – just before the pandemic began. In the car on the way home, she and the kids were trying to imagine a possible scenario where her three business revenues would dry up simultaneously. The three businesses – student rental units in university towns in Southern Ontario, school-based vending machines and royalties from school-based software – were like 'cash cows' that were seemingly insulated. They concluded that there was no way that an emergency fund was needed.

Then the pandemic hit. The post-secondary students didn't need housing in the university towns since schools pivoted to using on-line learning. The school-based vending machines weren't being used. The software royalties dipped.

She remembered my urging – 'set up an emergency fund' – and vowed that when she was on the other side of her personal journey through the pandemic's economic chaos, she would give me a call to tell me that I was 100% correct. She came out of her personal crisis – entrepreneurs are so often wired to find a way – and made that call. She urged me to continue telling all my attendees to have an emergency fund. Learning from those that have struggled and persevered is often extremely wise.

Penny says...

You need an emergency fund – this is an absolute priority - and your credit card or your line of credit is NOT an emergency fund! Three to six months of net salary is an adequate emergency fund for each earner. Be sure to stretch it to six months if you are in an industry that is cyclical since slowdowns happen whether or not you are prepared.

You don't need 'new' and you certainly don't need 'best'!

Ground zero here is your vehicle, but more on that later.

Let's consider your cell phone. Don't roll over your model if it's working fine simply because you have had it for 24 months and you are now done paying it off monthly on your plan. Keep your phone – it likely is still working just fine – and watch your monthly payments drop. When it is time to get a new phone, you don't need the newest version. Last year's model will be on promotion for $0 down, so choose it. As mentioned, make it a habit to call your service providers on a regular basis to check for better rates. They want to keep your business and the monthly cash flow is critical to them; they will negotiate with you to keep the revenue flowing.

Consider buying high-quality refurbished electronics. Picking up a high-end laptop that was returned for some reason, and then refurbished, can translate into saving 70% off the purchase price when compared to the cost of a new model.

When it comes to sports equipment for you or the kids, buying used gear is the way to go. From used skates for the kids who outgrow two pairs a year to used or 'demo' golf clubs for you, the price savings can again be in the 70% range. The same applies for home maintenance equipment, such as snowblowers or lawnmowers!

Before you go shopping for new appliances, check out local 'scratch and dent' options. The selection can be surprisingly broad and the cost savings versus 'new' will make the time worthwhile.

If you do want to buy 'new', you don't need 'best'. For big ticket items, scan the reviews and go with a quality product. Recognize that premium pricing often doesn't actually equate to the most reliable, best product. Don't be 'brand fixated'. A no-name coffee maker might be just as good as a designer coffee maker that is endorsed by a celebrity, but it likely has a price tag that is more appealing than that of the brand name product.

Before you buy something that's new, consider whether or not it makes any sense to search an on-line classified site first. Has one of the kids outgrown a smaller bed? Finding a used bedframe might be effortless and save you half the cost. Add a new mattress and you're all set.

Done with it? Get rid of it!

Items get replaced. Often, the item that we had originally is still in fine shape. Sell it now! Don't store it! Don't tell yourself you will sell it later. Sell it now! The benefits? Well, first of all, you don't have to store the item. Secondly, it will just keep going down in value as time passes. Thirdly, look at this strategy as a way of decreasing the net cost of the new item. Win, win, win! Want an equally good solution? Donate that item – thank it for its good service and send it on its way! As mentioned earlier, this is a great way to avoid the personal stress that comes with being surrounded by clutter – code for 'stuff' – in our homes! The self-storage rental facility industry is booming in Canada because some feel that the best way to deal with all their stuff is just to rent some more space. Here's a great alternative – plan to rid yourself of possessions that become obsolete.

Be at the table when the money decisions involving you are made!

Couples divvy up household responsibilities all the time. Given the hectic pace of modern-day living, that's a good way to cope and make sure all the balls stay in the air. When it comes to financial matters, someone has to take the lead so that the bills all get paid on time and accounts keep minimum balances. Having said that, both partners must stay informed regarding the financial status of the household. This is especially true when it comes to making investment decisions. Shared decision making allows all stakeholders to have a say in the decisions and understand the progress that's being made to achieve goals. For example, if a couple is trying to accumulate $100,000 for a down payment for a home, that involves lots of sacrificing. As mentioned, scheduling weekly or monthly check-in meetings provides an opportunity to encourage one another and feel good together about the progress that is being made. If you work with a financial advisor, schedule quarterly review meetings.

This shared responsibility also allows all involved to understand the process, and this can decrease the financial anxiety that comes with being confused about your shared financial situation.

Penny says...

No one should care about your money more than you. You need to take responsibility for how your money is managed and invested. If others are managing your money for you, stay involved in the process and ask questions until you understand what's happening. You have to be at the table here.

Big Banks don't work for you!

Realizing that you need help with your finances and taking steps to get the help you need is wise. Don't totally abdicate financial responsibility for your life to anyone, though; keep informed about your finances if you delegate responsibility to a partner or a financial professional. Realize, though, that turning to a Big Bank for financial advice has drawbacks.

Every country needs strong banks, and the alternative is disastrous for any nation's entire economy. Our Big Banks are economic powerhouses which is a good thing but, frankly, the Big Banks don't work for you. They are motivated to earn ever-rising profits (e.g., billions and billions of dollars each quarter) and they are tremendously good at it! We all have a vested interest in the banks remaining profitable since they are a tremendous source of credit for many Canadians, and we all have an indirect ownership of them through the Canada Pension Plan (CPP). However, recognizing how the Big Banks are earning billions of dollars in profits is sobering.

Big Bank staff members are trained to offer products that do NOT put your needs ahead of profits. Do an e-search for 'Big Bank staff members under pressure to sell' and see what you find; not only are they trained to do this, they are under pressure to do it. Want an example? Canadians have massive amounts of money invested in Big Bank mutual funds when there are far, far better options available. These mutual funds have very high fees. These high fees sabotage long-term results. Ask yourself why so many Canadians invest in these funds if there are better choices, even amongst the Big Bank offerings. Banks are very, very good at earning massive profits!

Penny says...

Bank branches are often called retail locations in the industry for a reason; financial products are sold there. Buying these products may not always be in your best interest. Keep a close eye on fees associated with any Big Bank investment product, since there are likely much cheaper alternatives elsewhere.

But credit unions do!

Want an alternative to the Big Banks? Consider the country's many credit unions! They are owned by their members. That's right – when you become a credit union client, you become an owner with an equal say in how the credit union operates, and this difference matters. Canada's credit unions have consistently ranked first in overall customer service excellence across all Canadian financial institutions for many, many years now.[6] Credit union offerings also span the financial landscape to meet the needs of both consumers and businesses. Simply put, they are a great alternative when compared to the Big Banks!

Minimizing your banking fees can be a 'win-win' move!

Minimize your banking fees. Low is good. Zero is better. This likely means you need to be a client of a virtual bank or keep a minimum balance in a Big Bank or credit union chequing or savings account to avoid monthly service fees and account activity charges. Big Banks have cranked these minimum balances up dramatically. Despite this, plan to maintain the minimum balance and view this as 'win-win': you will avoid paying hefty banking fees, and you will have an emergency fund in place, too.

Actively search out a financial mentor!

Life is challenging. If it's not right now, it will be someday. Storms are coming. We all need help. We all need to talk things out. This isn't a sign of weakness – it's actually just the opposite. Mental health is now something that is talked about openly. Businesses are much more attuned to the mental health of their workforce. It's the right thing to do, but it is also good for business.

Since we know that financial worries top the list of stressors for Canadians, one of the top strategies for you to action is ensuring that you have financial mentor. Who is guiding you financially? Who is checking your thinking around your financial goals? Who is nudging you to make changes in your spending patterns if they are not aligned with your financial goals?

We all know that having valued mentors in our life is a blessing because life is full of challenges. Surely, it makes sense to have a mentor in place to help you with your financial challenges!

Seek out a competent financial advisor to fill this role. Check their references, and ask your connections who have their financial house in order to provide a referral for their financial advisor.

Penny says...

Folks hesitate to pay for financial advice. This is foolish. You wouldn't expect your automotive mechanic to fix your car for free, so you shouldn't hesitate when it comes to paying for financial advice. Be sure the fee is transparent so that you know what you are paying and what you will be receiving!

Working with a financial advisor will lead to better results but...

Surveys show that investor results improve when working with a financial advisor.[7] This is intuitive – your car probably will run better if you take it to a mechanic than if you try to repair it yourself, or don't maintain it whatsoever. Financial advisors have the expertise and training to guide clients with their investment decisions. Trusted financial advisors really earn their keep when stock markets are volatile and investors may be tempted to make decisions driven by fear and greed.

How are they compensated? Typically, financial advisors earn a commission when they sell financial products. Some earn a set fee – usually 0.5% - 1% of assets under management – for managing your portfolio. Others provide 'fee for service' where they will undertake financial advising and bill you for their time. The challenge for small investors is that these structures may not generate enough in fees for a financial advisor to take them on as a client. This is another reason why so many small investors turn to Big Banks for investing advice. There are better alternatives – more on this later.

Once your portfolio is large enough (e.g., a minimum of six figures), you should be seeking the advice of a financial advisor, even if you only require another set of eyes to look over your portfolio. Ideally, they should possess a professional qualification that requires them to operate with a fiduciary responsibility to put client needs above all else.

Penny says...

Here's the one key question to ask a financial advisor after each quarter: Did my investments outperform the market indices this period? If the answer is 'no' on a consistent basis, then push hard to have your investments deployed in such a way to mimic the market indices, which should lead to much, much lower fees. This concept is explored in much greater detail in 'Part III - Mastering Investing'.

Taxes are taxing – get them done anyway!

File your personal income tax return. File it on time, file it every year and pay any taxes owing. Report all income, and be sure to claim only expenses that are allowable.

Depending on your circumstances, using one of the leading income tax software products that is widely available in Canada is just fine. If your return is more complex (e.g., small business ownership), consulting with a tax expert in order to prepare your returns both now and in the future is wise. Know your accountant's name and view yourself as a long-term client. Your accountant will understand your circumstances and can add value to the income tax process since this professional will suggest steps you can take to legally lower your taxes going forward, once you enter into that conversation.

Don't think you need to bother getting your income taxes filed? Try getting a mortgage without filing your taxes! Lenders will confirm your income. They do this by checking your Canada Revenue Agency (CRA) 'Notice of Assessment'. You get one of these after you have submitted your personal tax return and it has been assessed by CRA. Good luck, too, with getting a mortgage with an overdue amount owed to CRA!

Realize that lenders examine income to determine if you can carry a mortgage. If you are self-employed, you may feel tempted to not report all of your income for a variety of reasons. In sectors where 'paying cash' is common, these temptations are real. It's important to understand that if you make it a practice to 'low ball' income and write off expenses aggressively year after year to lower both your net income and your income taxes payable, you may be hampering your odds of getting a mortgage. For those mortgage applicants that are self-employed, mortgage lenders understand that income can vary, so they often calculate the average of the last two years' self-employment income. If a lender sees that the current year's income is below that average or that the two-year average is low, they will question where the money is going to come from to pay off the mortgage. Keep this in mind when it comes time to prepare your personal income taxes when a mortgage or mortgage renewal is in your future.

Much more on taxes as they relate to investing in 'Part IV – Mastering Your RRSP, RESP & TFSA'.

Penny says...

Personal income tax is just one type of tax that we pay, and we are heavily taxed in this area. Having said that, lashing back at the system by not filing a personal income tax return annually is not in your best interest. File your personal income tax return on time each year, and be sure to pay any income taxes owing by the deadline. Your future self will thank you for following this guidance.

Have a workplace benefit plan or a workplace pension plan? Understand them!

We often focus on the headline salary figure or wage amount when thinking about employment compensation. That's certainly important but a workplace benefit plan is very important, too. If you have one, get to know it better. If you don't have one, you will need to consider acquiring insurance to make up for the deficiency. Costs such as dental care, eye wear, orthodontic work for the kids (if applicable), massage treatments and physiotherapist treatments can add up very, very quickly. So, too, can prescription drug costs, which are certainly not all covered by provincial health insurance plans. Having some (or all) of these expenses covered by a workplace benefit program is a huge help financially.

If you are member of a workplace pension plan (also called a 'registered pension plan'), understanding the difference between a defined benefit (DB) pension plan and a defined contribution (DC) pension plan is important. With a DB plan, you can calculate your pension and when you will be eligible to retire by referencing a formula that's part of the plan (thus the name 'defined benefit'). Typically, the variables will include your years of work (or service) and your age totalling to a certain number, which will tell you when you are eligible to retire on a workplace pension with no reductions. To calculate the dollar amount of your pension, you typically use your years of service, multiplied by a factor (say 2%) to get a percentage, and then multiply that percentage by some type of average salary figure. This should all be set out in your workplace contract and perhaps collective agreement.

Here's an example of a DB plan for illustrative purposes.

• Let's say there's an employee who started working full-time for an organization at the age of 25, and worked for 30 years with an employer DB pension plan that has an '85 factor'

• After 30 years of full-time work, the employee would be 55 years of age

• At that age and with that many years of full-time work, the employee would have reached the '85 factor' (age plus years of service = 55 + 30 = 85) and be eligible for an unreduced pension

• The dollar amount would be arrived at by taking years of service (30) times a stated factor (say 2%, per the collective agreement) to get a percentage (30*2% = 60%)

• That percentage is multiplied by an average salary figure (let's say it is the employee's 'best five years' of annual salaries which might be $80,000) for a pension amount of $48,000 (60%*$80,000)

• This amount is often then adjusted annually while taking inflation into account with limits that are determined by factors such as the financial health of the pension plan

DC plans are very different. With DC plans, the employer makes no promises as to the future pension amount. The employer and the employee contribute set amounts (thus the name 'defined contribution'), and then the employee makes decisions about how this pool of money is invested, given a range of plan choices. The employee owns the investment decisions and inherits the consequences that come with that. The employee should definitely seek out professional advice to assist with these decisions.

If you are a member of a DC or DB workplace pension plan, consider buying back any service credit time related to leaves, including parental leaves, if applicable – more on this in 'But I have a workplace pension plan – so I don't have to worry about money, right?', which is found in Part IV.

In addition, if you are significantly younger than your partner and you are both members of a workplace pension plan, consider continuing to work as opposed to retiring when your older partner retires since the penalties for early retirement can be significant. For example, a typical penalty might be in the range of approximately 2.5% for every point short of the retirement factor, which could translate into a 5% reduction in annual pension income for retiring one calendar year before you reach your unreduced retirement date. That will hurt.

Workplace pension plans typically work in concert with CPP and Old Age Security (OAS) payments. Consult your tax advisor for further assistance here.

You may be able to commute the value of your workplace pension. This involves taking a lump sum before a certain age is reached in lieu of future pension payments. There would be reasons to do this, such as a terminal illness resulting in you facing a shortened life expectancy. However, if you encounter a financial advisor who encourages you to commute your pension so that the advisor can help you reach for better investment returns, you should walk away quickly. Don't underestimate the peace of mind that comes with a workplace pension plan!

Be intentional about protecting your most valuable asset!

What's your most valuable asset? Perhaps you might answer that it's your home if you own one or your investment portfolio. What about the person in the mirror? If you planted a 'money tree' in the backyard and it produced a crop of $3,000 to $4,000 each month, wouldn't you consider buying some type of insurance to protect that monthly income? Well, that 'money tree' is you! (Sorry, there really is no 'money tree'!) Make no mistake – YOUR earning potential is your most valuable asset. It needs to be protected for your sake, and the sake of your family if others depend on your income to cover living costs.

Understand if your workplace benefit plan comes with life insurance and disability insurance coverage. If your plan doesn't include those components or if you don't have a workplace benefit plan, get some advice from an insurance agent who will offer you options here.

Make it a priority to have adequate insurance in place. You must manage the financial risks in your life because they are real. Life is filled with uncertainty, but having an appropriate product such as life insurance provides the ability to ensure your family's financial security. Having no coverage (or inadequate coverage) to protect you and your family is like disregarding the toll that a financial calamity would inflict on you and your loved ones.

'Group life insurance plans' are widely advertised. Be cautious here; these plans may not be well suited to your individual needs. A life insurance agent can guide you through the process of ensuring that 'individual' coverage is in place, including recommending an appropriate amount of coverage. These 'individual' policies can be tailored to your specific needs so as to ensure that the coverage provided will be comprehensive, complete and appropriate, given your unique circumstances.

Penny says...

Financial advisors recommend that an individual have total life insurance coverage equal to approximately eight to twelve times their annual income. The exact amount depends on variables, such as the number of dependents, outstanding debt and personal preferences around how to provide for family in the event of premature death. 'Term insurance' coverage can often be purchased for a surprisingly small monthly premium. Consulting with a life insurance agent is wise given the importance of these decisions.

"I want to go on vacation but they are so ridiculously expensive!" They don't have to be...

Travelling and vacationing are special experiences. They bring a wonderful change of pace into our lives and broaden our world perspective. Unfortunately, for many people, they become financial nightmares because of out-of-control spending, and the debt that often comes with that. Here's a list of strategies and tips that will allow you to vacation more often without the debt hangovers that can greet you when you get back home.

• Autosave after each payday for vacations if they are a priority for you (you must have seen that one coming!)

• Never put a vacation on a credit card if you can't pay off the whole balance next month

• Be realistic about your vacation plans given the current state of your finances

• Skip the all-inclusive resorts and cruises unless you can afford them since so much of the charge goes to covering your food and adult beverage bill, and all-you-can-eat buffets are just code for 'overeating happens here'

• Efficiency suites or condos can be more expensive than hotel rooms, but they come with kitchens/kitchenettes which will allow you to avoid eating out for every meal

• Cut your meal bill significantly by committing to buy groceries for breakfast and lunch

> o Buying a special breakfast cereal for the kids can make these meals a treat for them, too

• Don't eat at a restaurant each night; bring in dinner a few times during the vacation to control expenses

• Consider driving as opposed to flying, especially if you are booking for a family (airfare is expensive and flying also involves renting a car)

• Considering a special family experience such as visiting some theme parks in the sunny south? By all means, go for it but, again, don't view your budget as being unlimited! Perhaps spend two days in the parks as opposed to seven; the kids won't remember the last five days anyway!

• Consider destinations within a day's drive in Canada to maximize time for fun, cut travel expenses significantly and eliminate worrying about a weak Canadian dollar wreaking havoc on your vacation budget

- If dollars are tight, destinations closer to home also allow you to perhaps go for three or five days as opposed to a week or more, which means that you get to pack in lots of fun in a shorter period of time

- Seasonal camping offers great family fun and, once you have the gear bought, you can lower your accommodation costs when compared to resort and hotel charges

- Booking a Saturday night hotel stay at a nearby destination is an inexpensive way to create two days of weekend memories

- Day trips are awesome ways to enjoy all of our wonderful outdoor activities – just remember to pack some snacks for the car and for when you hit the beach or the hiking trails

Eating habits can often be abandoned during vacations and short getaways. Make an effort to follow the outlined mealtime strategies and tips as a way to maintain some type of routine while away from home. This is especially important when it comes to travelling with the kids; if you screw the kids' routine up, that will screw your vacation up!

Penny says...

Vacations can provide lifelong memories; they are fertile ground for the 'spend time on experiences as opposed to buying stuff' mantra! Be sure to autosave for them!

Toys, toys, toys...

'Whoever has the biggest toys, wins' is plain silly, financially. Big toys like boats or motorhomes are extremely expensive to buy, and usually bring with them more debt. They certainly have major upkeep costs and depreciate quickly. You have to figure out storage too.

I once read that the two best days for any boat owner as related to their boat are the day the boat is bought and the day they get rid of it. That seems a bit harsh, but you get the point.

'Keeping up with the boys' or 'keeping up with the girls' can often be the motivation here. Consider renting any of these toys as opposed to buying them. This works wonderfully for smaller toys too, such as jet skis. You can enjoy all the benefits without being saddled with the associated debt.

But I want a cottage!

Everyone wants a cottage – during the summer, when the weather is perfect. Everyone wants a chalet – during the winter, when the weather is perfect.

Ever feel like you have trouble keeping up with the maintenance where you live now? How would you find the time or energy to maintain multiple properties? A friend once described owning a summer cottage like this: "We love the cottage but when we are up there, we feel as if we should be home, and when we are home, we feel like we should be up at the cottage." Doesn't that sound like fun?

Vacation properties such as cottages and chalets are similar to big toys except that they come with further upkeep costs, but have the allure of entertainment and price appreciation. While any profits (capital gains) from the sale of your primary residence are tax free, that's not the case with additional properties that you own. When it comes to any additional properties, any capital gains are taxable.

Renting vacation properties is the way to go for the vast majority of people because you just walk away from all the headaches that accompany vacation property ownership while enjoying the benefits when you are on vacation. It also allows maximum flexibility when it comes time to your vacation decisions, both from a location perspective but also when viewed through a seasonal lens. Heading to a Canadian cottage during December likely isn't too appealing, if you are looking for a break from our winter weather.

If you do decide to purchase a vacation property, consider renting it out when you are not using it, so as to bring in additional revenue. Consult a tax expert here for direction around expensing costs associated with the property, which could offset the tax you will pay on the rental income.

Penny says...

If you have visited a popular tourist destination, you have likely been personally invited to a timeshare presentation. You are offered the promise of receiving a perk, such as free tickets to a popular local tourist attraction, in exchange for giving up a few hours of your vacation time to attend the presentation. Keep your wits about you if you decide to attend one of these presentations. These are effective, high-pressure, professional sales events that have been designed to get you to commit on the spot to significant future costs around vacationing. Making major, unexpected financial commitments while under duress sets the table for lots of regret.

With a little effort, you can save a lot of money on ongoing household expenses!

It's wise to know the difference between household projects that you can handle yourself and those that need a professional to complete. Your property is valuable and maintaining it is really a non-negotiable. Know when you can do something yourself (e.g., changing the furnace filter) and know when to call in an expert (e.g., electrical work).

Savings can be had when considering your regular household expenses.

Your ongoing household bills tell a story. Be aware of your bills and take steps to keep costs – such as charges for electricity, gas and water usage – under control. You might not be aware that a toilet is leaking, but it can cause your water bill to spike. Catching it sooner than later saves money, and a dollar saved is a dollar earned. With home costs, you can add a bunch of zeros behind that dollar!

Heating and cooling costs are likely at the very top of your home's household expenses so taking steps to curb these costs is wise.

Be sure that you have a programmable thermostat or a smart thermostat in your house. Lower your home's temperature during heating season when you are not home, and at night. Turn down the furnace to the point that you are comfortable wearing a sweater in the house during the day when you are home. Have a few soft, cozy blankets around your living space to grab when enjoying some screen time. Similar steps can be taken during air conditioning season, too. Yes, use your AC when needed but, if you have a basement that stays cool, consider running your furnace's fan as opposed to running the air conditioner continuously. During warm summer days, this will allow the cooler air in the basement to circulate throughout the house. Open up the windows, when reasonable, to help heat and cool your home when Mother Nature co-operates.

Pay attention to 'time of day' pricing for electricity usage, and keep those times posted on your fridge so you can easily see the specifics on a regular basis. Delay running the washer, dryer and dishwasher to avoid peak hours. Turn down your water heater's hot water setting a notch, too. Don't put off dealing with anything that is leaking; toilets, faucets and shower heads that are dripping will drain your wallet too. Upgrade your lighting to LED bulbs. Use light timers when you are away from home to avoid keeping lights on for extended periods of time while still giving the impression that someone is in the house.

Get a clothesline for drying laundry, and use it!

Wait until 'end of season' when possible, to capture deeper discounts on virtually all home items, from your winter maintenance needs to your summer maintenance needs and home décor items too. Buying new beach chairs in August as opposed to May would be a great example.

Be sure to maximize your household recycling and composting. It's the right thing to do for the environment and, depending on where you live, paying for tags to place on excess garbage bags is a reality now, or will be coming soon.

Want a top tip for extending your furnace's life? Change the filter furnace as recommended. Do this during all seasons too. Put reminders on your phone, and keep filters on hand so that you can change them on schedule. Be sure to also seal drafty doors and windows to cut your energy usage charges.

Smart home devices can certainly help you control many parts of your home beyond the heating and cooling system. For example, appliances and security system components can now communicate, and this 'Internet of Things' trend will only accelerate as time moves on.

Following tips such as these will pay off immediately and will create ongoing savings!

Want to make some of your housing costs tax deductible? Read on...

The pandemic certainly brought on (or accelerated) significant labour market shifts. One of those was the prevalence of working from home. The gig economy has also allowed many to tap into their entrepreneurial spirit and open home-based businesses as a side hustle, or as a primary source of income. Many homes are already set up with the technology to make a home-based business feasible, and the arrival of virtual meeting platforms has removed the last real barrier to making working from home a legitimate option for many. These are megatrends that aren't going away anytime soon; more people are going to be working from home than was the norm in the 2010s.

In addition to the savings generated by not needing to physically travel to work, there also comes the possibility of taking a portion of your housing costs and expensing them. The CRA states that these deductions (such as electricity, heating and maintenance) must be reasonable, and are typically calculated by examining the portion of your home's living space that is used for business purposes. Records need to be kept (for CRA tax audit purposes) to back up any of these expenses and, if you are required to work from home by your employer, confirmation of that needs to be provided by your employer. In the midst of the pandemic, CRA introduced a new temporary flat rate method designed to simplify the process for claiming home office expenses for employees. Given the emerging 'work from home' trend, expect this temporary change to have some staying power. It may be worth turning to a tax professional for additional direction and guidance here, given the option of going with the flat rate method or the detailed method, which involves some calculations.

Consider starting a home-based job as a side hustle to not only bring in more income, but to also take advantage of CRA tax write-off opportunities, as related to allowable home expenses.

Going to restaurants should be viewed as a treat rather than the default option for meals

Go to the grocery store or your favourite neighbourhood market and buy healthy, nutritious food for your meals – but make a list first and don't go grocery shopping when you are hungry! Buy what's in season and do this all year long. Work the perimeter of the grocery store first – that's where the fruits, vegetables, dairy and protein are found. Beware of anything that comes in a box or a can because that likely means that the contents were processed. Plan your grocery shopping and be a 'virtual coupon clipper' or an 'on-line price matcher', if that works for you. Make every effort to avoid realizing at the end of the workday that you have no idea what's for dinner. This leads to constantly having meals delivered or picking up fast food on the way home. It's not a healthy option and it's unbelievably expensive compared to buying groceries. By the way, 'going to a restaurant' can also mean bringing something home since buying any type of drink at any restaurant is ridiculously expensive! There's nothing wrong with bringing a pizza home, but have a homemade salad with it; it's healthier and cheaper, too.

Shop at a local farmers' market, if possible. The abundance and quality of fresh fruit and vegetables will encourage you to eat more of these healthy choices. The items will be fresher and will last longer, decreasing your food waste costs. You will also be supporting your local economy, which is an added bonus.

Speaking of food waste, get in the habit of 'rotating stock' when it comes to the way you manage and store perishable food items, such as fruits, vegetables, dairy products, breads and meats. There's solid thinking behind why large grocery stores load milk into the back of their large commercial display fridges. It's called FIFO – first in, first out – and it's a conscious effort on the part of your grocer to sell older items first. Follow the same formula, and make sure you rotate your canned and boxed foods too; they also have 'best before' dates.

Eat breakfast at home as opposed to ordering a breakfast sandwich combo at the drive-thru five times a week. Pack your lunch – do it! This provides great role modelling opportunities for kids, by the way. Couples need to be on the same page here, too, or there will be friction; having one partner 'brown bagging it' while the other one goes out for lunch each day is going to be a sore spot eventually.

Penny says...

Get in the habit of looking over your upcoming week every Sunday night so as to map out the coming days. That's the time to spot the pressure points and make a plan regarding meals. Always have a few healthy frozen entrees in the freezer that you can pull out when life invariably throws a curve ball at you when it comes time for nightly meal preparation.

Find free (or almost free) fun!

There are many, many free or relatively inexpensive activities that you can enjoy without breaking the piggybank. Many can be done by yourself or with others too.

Walk! Walking has proven to be one of the healthiest activities that you can possibly do, and the mental health benefits of being outdoors are tangible, also. As a matter of fact, many outdoor activities have similar attributes. From riding a bike to going for a run to doing yoga in the park to doing some hiking, being outside is just plain fun, and none of these activities are overly expensive!

Fitness club memberships, on the other hand, are expensive. Think of alternatives. Cardio workouts can be easily done outside when the weather is agreeable. Picking up a used pair of cross-country skis or a pair of snowshoes or ice skates is a great way to give yourself outdoor wintertime exercise options too. You don't need to invest in an expensive home gym. Using your own body weight to do strength work is often much safer on your body than lifting heavy weights. The number of on-line workouts that are available is staggering, and you can certainly pursue any of these fitness activities with a friend or family member to gain the benefits of social time and camaraderie, too. By the way, don't buy bottled water, nor expensive sports drinks – get a good water bottle and use it!

Have you been in your local public library lately? Libraries have changed significantly and now often offer a wonderful assortment of workshop and speaker presentations at no charge. The resource selection is, of course, outstanding.

Your local community likely offers a wide variety of activities through the Parks & Recreation Department that are definitely worth considering. From access to indoor and outdoor community pools to drop-in basketball, badminton, floor hockey or volleyball to arts and crafts sessions, the offerings are superb and the costs are minimal.

Are you a sports fan? Consider catching local high school or university games. Rep sports are also very entertaining to watch. We are in Canada so lower-level junior hockey games are plentiful and entertaining. The calibre of play is often outstanding, and the costs to attend are a fraction of what you would pay to catch a pro game or even a major junior hockey game. If you do attend a live professional sports event, examine the pricing plans. Attending a tennis or golf tournament earlier in the week or a major junior hockey game on a weeknight will likely be less expensive than catching weekend action since dynamic pricing models are now becoming common for both sports and cultural events. It goes without saying that there's no value in buying the best seats in the house. Expect food and drink prices to be exorbitant, so having a meal before arriving at the venue makes perfect sense.

Attending free local and regional outdoor festivals is a tremendous way to spend quality time with family and friends while enjoying all that this beautiful country has to offer.

Streaming services and cable are entertainment sources too, as are subscriptions for magazines and newspapers. Be sure you are getting the use out of them to justify the costs. Bundle services whenever possible since there are significant savings when internet costs are added in. Drop the telephone landline – you don't need it – and be sure that you are getting the data that you need for your smartphone to avoid overage charges.

By the way, spending money on smoking, vaping, marijuana or excessive drinking isn't in your best interest from either a health or financial perspective. Trim this spending and re-direct the money to savings – you'll never regret it on many levels!

Penny says...

Health is the #1 wealth! You don't have to spend a lot of money to keep fit but you do need to keep moving! Your future self will thank you for investing time on yourself in this area!

"I just got a raise! Time to spend it!" NOPE!

Save the raise or use it to pay down high-interest debt like credit card debt or student loans. Divert as much of the raise as you can (e.g., 90%) to your savings buckets or debt repayment. If it is a lump sum bonus, save all of it and immediately get it out of your operating account and into your virtual bank savings buckets.

Never count on raises. Spending a raise on a vacation and then being shocked when the raise (or promotion) doesn't come your way is a double shot to the gut.

If you are in a public service sector, be extremely cautious around your expectations for pay raises going forward. With calm inflation and staggering government debt levels, governments might just not have the financial flexibility to offer significant pay increases to their public service sector workforce. Bargaining table offers featuring minimal pay increases are definitely a real possibility.

Planning on winning the lottery?

If you play long enough, you inevitably must win a big lottery prize, right? Well, here's a fact that might make you doubt that, as posted on the Ontario government agency website that manages the sale of province-wide lottery games:

"Consider this: The odds of winning the jackpot in a game like Lotto 6/49 are approximately 1 in 14 million, similar to the odds of putting the name of everyone in Ontario in a hat – a very tall hat – and randomly pulling out your own."[8]

Big numbers are hard to grasp. Let me see if I can help by walking through an exercise that I used in class to help my students comprehend huge numbers.

Let's imagine that you were able to do nothing but count for a very, very long time. Let's say that you were able to count one number per second, for every second of every day. You could, therefore, count to 86,400 in one day (60 seconds in a minute*60 minutes in an hour*24 hours in a day). At that rate, it would take you 162 days, which is well over five months, to get to 14 million.

Penny says...

Yes, someone is going to win the next big lottery but it's almost a certainty that it won't be you. 'Winning the lottery' can't be the plan when it comes to ensuring your financial freedom.

In life, managing expectations matters – this is so true in your financial life!

Your first home isn't going to be your dream home but that's okay. It takes time. You are not going to immediately have amenities (such as a 75-inch TV and expensive, leather furniture) that your parents perhaps have now. You are not going to be able to afford a new car right out of school. Your vacations aren't going to be extravagant right off the bat.

You will have limited dollars despite creditors wanting to perhaps extend you access to large amounts of money through credit cards, lines of credit and mortgages. That's potential debt, and debt is a four-letter word.

In a cruel twist, just when you are launching and starting to enjoy financial independence, you need the most stuff – but have virtually no financial assets with which to finance those purchases. This is likely the case, for example, when it comes to furnishing your first condominium or getting your first car. The debt trap has been set and waits for you right here. Many get caught in this debt trap. They will even post the evidence on their social media accounts. Make no mistake – it's a trap.

You are going to have to rein in your expectations when it comes to your financial life. View your financial life like a book – it's a journey. You won't have everything you want in the first chapter, but with time you can reach your financial goals if you have a plan and follow it. If you don't set financial goals, you will have no idea where you are heading; you set yourself up to be 'lost' financially.

The reality is that the road to financial independence is simple to map out, if time is on your side – but, the self-discipline and self-regulation that are needed make the journey anything but easy. Expect it to be tough, and manage your expectations along the way.

Penny says...

You are going to have to prioritize spending since you are not going to have a money tree. As mentioned, there is no money tree. You are going to have to save for various purposes. If it's important to you, save for it. Accept that you will start with next to nothing, and have modest expectations as you launch.

Change is the constant...

Surprises will come along. Financial surprises certainly fall into that category, and sometimes those surprises are nasty ones. They could be on a micro-level (e.g., not getting that promotion nor the corresponding raise that you were expecting) or macro-level (e.g., a global financial crisis or global pandemic), but be sure that they are coming. They will impact your plans both financially and from a wellness perspective. They will cause duress. You will need to pivot. This doesn't mean you don't plan. What it means is that you view your plans as fluid.

Flexibility matters. Resiliency matters. Everyone struggles at times – everyone. Being able to roll with life's punches – financial punches, included – is a tremendous life skill and one that you will need many times in the future, often when you least expect it.

Penny says...

Shoot for excellence, not perfection, in all areas of your life. Take this view with your finances, too. You are not going to be 100% right all the time. Your investments will fall in value despite all of your planning. Stick to the plan and modify it when necessary. Keep going. Never give up. Be resilient. Your future self will thank you!

Give back!

Giving back is rewarding on so many levels! Share your good fortunes. Help others both financially, and by sharing your talents. Be generous. Make donating a part of your financial plan. Starting small is just fine. Automate your donating so that it becomes, well, automatic. Find causes that are near and dear to your heart and support those causes. Let that support grow year by year. There are countless reasons why this is a good idea; you know them all. Give back!

Guess what? You need a Will...

You can't say for certain 'when' you will need a Will, but you are going to need one. It needs to be professionally prepared because there's a lot on the line. It needs to be updated when a major life event occurs, such as having kids, acquiring real estate or getting married. Gather all of your key financial documentation in one spot – from bank and investment account numbers to insurance policy details to contact information for your lawyer, financial advisor and insurance agent – and tell the key people in your life where to find this information! Be sure to include virtual account numbers and login details too. These should all be reviewed annually with your significant other (if applicable).

Also, have the tough conversation with your parents regarding their Wills or anyone else who has asked you to take on the very serious responsibility of being an executor.

Rest assured that you're going to need a Will. Know, also, that your loved ones will be extremely appreciative that you followed through on this at some point in the future.

Penny says...

Expecting a big inheritance? Not so fast! Many more people are now entering retirement with substantial debt, including large mortgages. Those debts need to be paid off by the estate before any assets are distributed. In addition, Wills often contain 'surprises'. Don't plan on large inheritances to fund your retirement!

Post-secondary education costs are significant – so make a good decision!

Your career pathway choice begins with a journey inside to discover what you love to do! Once you have settled on the field that you love – and sometimes, this is all the clarity you have when you are younger – then it's time to make good decisions on how to get there. Realize that you often can put yourself in position to secure your dream job by following many different educational paths. Having said that, there are some factors to weigh carefully.

Broadly speaking, you have four post-secondary pathway options – directly enter the workforce, apprenticeship, college or university. Moving through your career with only a secondary school graduation diploma worked decades ago, but you will find this option will lead to chronic low paying jobs and low employment prospects. Invest in yourself and commit to one of the other options.

Post-secondary education costs are significant. It wouldn't be a surprise to see high-demand programs with lucrative future earning potential (e.g., business, engineering, medicine) raise tuition to 'user pay' levels.

If you are considering continuing with school, is there a local option available that would allow you to live at home? This puts you in position to significantly lower your post-secondary costs. Have an itch to move away from home? Consider programs with co-operative education or internship components. Not only do they provide supports for securing good paying jobs during non-school terms over the duration of your post-secondary school years, but they also allow you to 'test drive' your sector. Additionally, you are able to establish those crucial networks that can lead to countless opportunities as the years play out.

Be sure to have clarity around job prospects for grads from your program. Are you able to monetize your diploma/degree? Take steps (including volunteering) to not only gain experience to ensure that you are employable, but also to make sure that the field of work connected to your post-secondary training offers a good fit for you.

Penny says...

If possible, look to graduate debt-free after your first degree or diploma!

Apprenticeships offer great employment prospects along with job mobility!

If you love working with your hands and enjoy hands-on training, the skilled trades offer fantastic pathway options. Generally speaking, you will get paid while you complete your apprenticeship, so burdensome school debt likely isn't in your future. In addition, if you select a trade that is in demand, you will enjoy a steady stream of work opportunities over your career that pay well. Many of the skilled trades offer the possibility to 'be your own boss' once you gain experience. Commit to continuing your learning, and consider picking up some practical business training too, so that you are well-positioned if you do decide to branch out on your own.

College diploma programs, college applied degrees and graduate certificate programs can often open many doors for you!

Expect college programs to become more and more popular as a tremendous pathway option. The curriculum is grounded in practical application as opposed to theory. Class sizes are typically smaller, and tuition costs are significantly below those associated with university programs. Graduates often walk right into employment; the programs are often designed to align with employment needs. Many university graduates decide to complete college certificate programs to increase their marketability and job competitiveness. That, in and of itself, is a great testament to the quality of the programs offered by our colleges!

The university pathway is an expensive one so be sure your program is worth the investment!

For many jobs, a university degree is a requirement. However, look long and hard at the benefit of completing a given degree. University is expensive and costs will continue to skyrocket. Do your research. What are the job prospects and salary levels for recent graduates from this or that program? For some programs, the prospects are superb, but it's often tremendously difficult to earn a spot in these programs, and the academic pressure is ratcheted up during each and every semester. Also, many university students don't finish the program they start, or don't graduate at all.

Your earning potential and job prospects can be very, very bright as a university graduate if you earn a degree in the right program. It is certainly worth seeking out programs that have co-operative education components built right into the program. These can allow you to further gain an edge on your competition, and make a better choice once you enter the job market after graduation.

Key takeaways from 'Mastering the Money Mindset'

→ have an 'attitude of gratitude' so as to begin taking control of your financial life

→ be intentional about collecting memories (as opposed to 'stuff')

→ be a lifelong learner since this allows you to become an expert in your field, and boosts your earning potential

→ be a saver (as opposed to a spender) so that you can put yourself in position to reach all your financial goals

→ automate your savings

→ have frequent money conversations with your life partner (if applicable) so as to support one another on your shared financial journey

→ have an adequate emergency fund since financial storms will come

→ realize that you don't need 'new'

→ make it a priority to be involved in financial decision making on a regular basis, even if others (such as a financial advisor or your life partner) manage this piece of your life

→ understand that Big Banks don't work for you

→ have a trusted financial mentor

→ protect your most valuable asset – your future earning potential – with adequate insurance

→ manage your financial expectations so as to put yourself in position for long-term financial success

Part II

Mastering Debt

In 'Mastering Debt', we'll discuss, well, debt. Yes, it's a four-letter word. We all will carry debt at some point in our lives, so it's incredibly important to learn how to manage our debt properly. Unfortunately, for many, debt is a huge source of stress and anxiety. Lenders make money when we use debt, and many Canadians take on that debt with wild abandonment. It's toxic for many. It's a huge struggle to make good financial decisions if you are weighed down by crushing debt. Getting a handle on debt will provide you with financial stability. There is no financial wellness without proper debt management.

Crucial lessons in this part of the book include the importance of improving your credit score, using credit cards wisely, and understanding the difference between 'good debt' and 'bad debt'.

Debt controls you or you control your debt – there's seldom a middle ground. The key lessons found here will allow you take control of your debt.

Canadians are addicted to debt, eh!

You've heard of the phrase 'death and taxes' before. They are held out as two givens in life. Perhaps that should be changed to 'debt, death and taxes' for those living here in the Great White North! Canadian consumers just keep heaping on the debt. We are addicted to it. We're in the midst of a silent national debt-fueled personal finance crisis that continues to play out in every corner of the country.

We all need to understand how we got here to change this story going forward.

How did we get on the 'debt train'?

What caused this silent national debt-fueled personal finance crisis? There are many factors at play, but here are some key ones:

- Slow wage growth

- Historic low interest rates

- Automation

- Our desire to keep up with our neighbours

- Unexpected economic shocks

- Lack of mandatory personal financial literacy taught in our schools

Wage growth has been very, very slow since the 2008-2009 financial crisis. Costs have been rising, though. Families have turned to debt to bridge the gap between their spending and their income.

Interest rates have been slashed by central banks around the world to record lows and are even negative in some countries. The powerful, closely-watched US central bank – the Federal Reserve – has even publicly shifted its priorities such that it will make taking action to push unemployment rates down its top priority. In order to do that, the 'Fed' acknowledged that it would not necessarily raise US interest rates when inflation topped the target rate of 2%. This has been interpreted as an acknowledgement that low interest rates are likely to be commonplace for quite some time. The reality is that federal governments are now carrying such massive debt that a return to a high interest rate environment would be catastrophic for developed countries. Low interest rates create the allure of debt being 'free money'.

In developed countries, the pace of automation has obliterated employment levels in manufacturing sectors, and has caused disruptions to employment in virtually all other sectors, too. Lower-paying service jobs have filled the void with families turning to debt to maintain their previous lifestyles.

We have an ingrained thirst to keep up with neighbours, and social media has made it painfully easy to see all the exciting things that others are buying and doing. FOMO – fear of missing out – is very powerful and causes us to think that, if our friends deserve to go on fancy trips or get new expensive gadgets, we deserve that too – and so we turn to debt.

Major, unexpected economic shocks happen. Regardless of the trigger, these economic shocks are very disruptive. These shocks come in different forms. Sometimes, they are more like a standalone financial event (such as the financial crisis in 2008-2009). Sometimes, they are the collateral damage that comes with non-financial events (such as the pandemic). From an economic point of view, the pandemic – and the associated lockdowns – wreaked havoc on government budgets in Canada as emergency stimulus dollars flowed to many citizens and businesses to avoid what would most definitely have been

68

a colossal economic depression. The economic carnage wasn't evenly felt, though. For those businesses and their workers who were deemed 'essential', the pandemic brought economic prosperity. At the same time, travel restrictions and lockdowns made it difficult to spend those dollars. Many found that their bank accounts swelled. Business owners (such as restauranteurs) and those connected to industries like travel and tourism struggled to keep their businesses open. As a result, the pandemic created financial winners and financial losers; those most adversely hit turned to debt in an effort to make it through to the other side of the economic storm.

The lack of mandatory personal financial literacy that is taught in our schools has made people vulnerable to making catastrophic mistakes when it comes to money management. There's also a tendency to feel a level of embarrassment when it comes to not understanding even the most basic personal finance content, such as how a credit card works. This lack of personal financial literacy understanding, combined with embarrassment, leads people to avoid reaching out for financial help. Presto – turning to debt becomes a national pastime. When combined with hesitation to reach out for help in this area, you get a silent national debt-fueled personal finance crisis.

Generations of Canadians have not been taught mandatory personal financial literacy in our schools. Going forward, it's the only way that our future generations can get off the 'debt train'.

You probably haven't been taught this content either. It's not your fault. Read on to find ways to better take control of debt.

Sorry…what does 'debt' even mean???

You likely possess lots of tangible stuff that has value, such as a car or your tech items like laptops. These items that you own are called assets. You may have acquired these items with other people's money or used your own money or perhaps a combination of the two. Any of this borrowed money is called debt. Debt means 'amounts you owe'. When it comes to debt, we owe money to individuals or organizations like a Big Bank. Those monies are liabilities. These entities then become our creditors. We have to pay our debts – creditors can take action against you if you don't pay monies owed. Creditors are entitled to make money. If you borrow money for a car loan, you will end up paying back more than you borrowed. That extra cost is typically made up of interest charges and fees. The major piece is usually the interest charge. Interest charges are expressed as an annual interest rate. Borrowers, therefore, always want low interest rates. By the way, creditors prefer higher interest rates since that juices their returns. You can see that there would be conflicting preferences there. Lenders earn your business by keeping their interest rates competitive, so most lenders will offer similar interest rates for similar products to similar customers.

Having a lot of debt can be overwhelming since the payments seem to never end and can build and build as we take on new debt. The more debt we carry, the more our financial risk increases since a job shock or similar negative economic event can put us in a position where we can't make our debt payments. As mentioned, we have to pay back debts, so creditors are legally allowed to take measures to get their money back. Creditors can hire collection agencies to assist with debt collection, or creditors can actually sell the debt to those collection agencies. Creditors can take control of collateral that we put up to back a loan (such as a car for a car loan or even a house for a mortgage), and they can also sue to force repayment. Creditors can also push us into bankruptcy in order to get their money back. The same principles apply to debts that businesses carry too. We often view creditors as the cause of bankruptcies. Yes, creditors can force you into bankruptcy in an attempt to get their money back, but consumers and businesses are the ones that took on the debt that led to the bankruptcy. As such, taking on too much debt is the real root cause of bankruptcies.

They have to give me a credit card, right?

Nope…

Lenders make money by lending money. They also take on the risk that comes with lending money; that risk is that the borrower won't be able to pay the money back. Lenders take this risk very, very, very, very seriously, and they take steps to mitigate, or manage, that risk. This is why you must apply for credit. Lenders will assess whether or not they feel that you are 'risk worthy'.

Know that you are not entitled to get a loan nor a mortgage nor a credit card. You earn that privilege. Sometimes lenders will take on more risk in a given situation than normal, but that is balanced out by having many stronger borrowers. They pool all these risks to manage them. They are good at this. Lending is very, very profitable for businesses like our Big Banks. When they see troubles coming in the economy, they prudently set aside larger reserves to offset losses that come from bad debts. Think of this as a Big Bank emergency fund. By the way, our government heavily regulates and monitors our Big Banks to ensure that they have proper reserves in place at all times. It's one of the core reasons that our Big Banks came out of the 2008-2009 financial crisis relatively unscathed, while some major US banks actually didn't even survive.

Lenders love collateral!

There are lots of lenders actively recruiting new borrowers now; as noted, lenders make money by lending out money. They make money by charging interest rates that are higher than their cost of money. Lenders want to lend, and we need strong lenders. Remember, when a lender gives you a loan, that money is an asset to them. The asset is a 'receivable' for the lender since you are required to pay the debt back. The alternative is having weak banks that have all kinds of impaired assets (money loaned to non-paying borrowers whose ability to make loan payments is uncertain) or don't have enough reserves in place to ride out an economic storm. They stop lending when a crisis hits and that is globally catastrophic from an economic perspective. We need strong lenders – and they need borrowers.

Lenders love collateral. Collateral helps lenders mitigate risk. If a lender approves a car loan for a borrower and the loan agreement states that payments must be made or the lender takes ownership of the car, that car is the collateral. The lender can sell the car to get their money back (or some of it at least). That allows lenders to lend to more people because the collateral mitigates the risk for the lender.

Loans are easier to understand as soon as you understand collateral. You pay for the amount of the loan (principal) plus interest and fees. The interest will be expressed as an annual percentage rate. You will make payments on a regular basis – usually monthly – for a certain number of months until the loan's principal is repaid. At that point, the asset is yours 'free and clear', and the lender has no remaining legal rights connected to that asset. For example, once your mortgage is paid off, the lender will issue a mortgage discharge statement declaring that they no longer have any claim on that real estate.

Credit cards are a very, very common source of debt – more on this later on in this part of the book. There's no collateral behind a credit card, typically. You can also just get a loan from a bank without collateral.

Student loans have no collateral and can be issued by financial institutions or governments.

Mortgages are loans for a home or other piece of real estate. They come with a much longer (typically twenty-five years) amortization period, meaning the length of time you have to repay the loan. Mortgages amounts are typically hundreds of thousands of dollars so more time is needed to repay them. There's much more on this topic in 'Part VI – Mastering Real Estate'.

The cost of money – understanding interest rates

When it comes to our financial life journey, many people trundle through predictable financial life stages. In high school, you get a job and put your money in a Big Bank savings account. Those saving accounts typically paid interest each month but they don't now. When you get to your post-secondary years, the school debt arrives and it mounts when you move out on your own. Then you buy real estate; that debt lasts for decades. When you finally do pay off all the debts or at least make a dent in paying them off, then you start saving for retirement. At about that time, you also try to help the kids with their schooling costs or perhaps with a down payment for their first real estate purchase.

This is what it looks like for many people. Basically, when you are carrying debts, you want low interest rates, and when you have money to invest, you want high interest rates. This means that, at any given time, many people are upset by interest rate levels.

There are two main types of interest rates – short-term and long-term. The government central banks around the world basically set short-term interest rates, and long-term interest rates are set by market forces in the bond market – more on this later when we look at variable-rate mortgages versus fixed-rate mortgages in 'Part VI – Mastering Real Estate'.

One of the core types of income for Big Banks is called 'net interest income'. It's calculated by taking the revenue banks earn by charging interest on products like mortgages or car loans and subtracting interest expenses that the banks pay on investments such as guaranteed investment certificates (GICs). Usually, the interest revenue that's brought in by longer-term products is higher than the interest expense that's paid out on shorter-term products. That's Banking 101 and it earns the Big Banks billions of dollars in profit.

Penny says...

While no one has a crystal ball, there is consensus amongst economists that we are going to be in a period of low interest rates for a prolonged period of time. This will not be good news for savers, but it will provide further incentive for consumers and businesses to borrow in order to help the economy recover from the double whammy that the 2008-2009 financial crisis and the COVID-19 pandemic inflicted on global economic growth. Governments will certainly count on low rates to affordably finance all of the new stimulus-related debt that the pandemic brought with it.

Your credit score matters…it matters a lot!

You have a credit score. That three-digit score also goes by the name 'beacon score' or 'FICO score' (named after the Fair Isaac Corporation that invented the credit scoring system). If you have a cell phone plan, you make monthly payments. Those plan providers track your payment patterns. If you have a credit card, those issuers track your payment patterns, too. The same tracking happens when you have a car loan or a mortgage.

We have two credit rating agencies in Canada – TransUnion Canada and Equifax Canada. You can contact them in order to access your credit report for free; that credit report contains your credit score. You can also subscribe to free services that will send you monthly credit score updates electronically. Your creditors report your payment history to these credit rating agencies on a frequent basis. These agencies then update your credit report and your credit score based on your history of managing credit. Credit reports contain all kinds of information, such as your outstanding loans, paid off loans, credit card balances and corresponding credit limits, lines of credit, employment history and address information, along with any previous bankruptcies, consumer proposals, court-ordered judgement and collection agency activities.[1]

Credit scores range from 300 to 900 and are derived from credit data in your credit report, such as your credit history and payment patterns. A score of over 750 is strong, and one in the low 600 range or below throws up red flags for creditors. Generally, lenders look for scores to be above 680 when it comes to offering preferred terms.

Checking your own personal credit score doesn't hurt your score, but applying for new credit, among other financial events, may cause your score to dip.

When you apply for any new credit, you will give permission for the potential creditor to not only check your credit score but also to report your payment history to the credit rating agencies if you become a client. You have probably consented to this many times in the past but it really never registers; the consent might even have been in the 'small print' just above the signature line. Your credit score seems like some abstract financial measurement tool that's just out there. It's real and it matters. A low credit score may block you from even qualifying for a loan, or it can put you in a great position where you are offered a special low interest rate on a mortgage. Clients with strong credit scores versus those with 'bruised credit' put themselves in position to qualify for lower interest rates on many types of credit products. Even a small difference in interest rates on a six-figure mortgage can equate to thousands and thousands of dollars worth of additional interest charges over the life of a mortgage.

Note that in Nova Scotia, Prince Edward Island and Saskatchewan, a business or individual isn't required to get your written consent in order to check your credit report; they just need to tell you that they are going to do this.[2]

It's wise to know your credit score and even wiser to know how it is calculated!

Time to make your credit score sexy!

The good news is that you can take steps to raise your credit score. Once you know how your score is calculated, you can be intentional about raising it! As mentioned, there are even some speed dating clubs that require you to bring your credit score. High credit scores are sexy!

Know that the way that you have managed your credit in the past, along with your current credit situation, are monitored by those credit rating agencies. You have to establish a 'track record' of good credit management in order to raise your credit score.

Your previous payment history carries a large weighting, so set up all bills on autopay. Pay off your balances every month; set the payments to 'full balances' as opposed to the 'minimum payment' amounts. Having a dispute with your cell phone provider over this month's payment? Paying late or missing payments will negatively impact your credit score. Pay the bill on time, and contact the cell phone provider's customer loyalty department – they want to keep your business and will negotiate in order to do so.

Your current level of indebtedness is highly weighted, too. Take action here. For example, don't keep your credit card balances anywhere near their limit. Shoot to keep your balances below 30% of your credit limit. More on this in 'As long as I don't go over my credit card limit, I'm in good shape, right? Wrong!', which is found later in this part of the book.

The actual length of credit history is a factor too, so apply for a credit card, use it and pay it off. Then, at the very least, use it from time to time to maintain that history.

Applying for multiple credit accounts in a short period of time will damage your score, so be careful here. You might want to think twice about applying for that new credit card at that hockey game so as to get the free team jersey, for example.

Having a healthy mix of credit accounts – like credit cards, retail accounts (such as store credit cards), lines of credit and a mortgage – shows 'credit maturity', which is an important piece of your credit profile.

Penny says...

Once you have a high credit score, it puts you in a position of power when it comes to negotiating with lenders. Unfortunately, the opposite is also true. Monitor your credit score, and consistently take steps to improve it! Your future self will thank you for it and, remember, a high credit score is sexy! Penny loves that one!

A.P.R. O.A.C. – help!

You likely have seen this set of letters before. They often appear in auto manufacturer advertisements, for instance. They stand for 'annual percentage rate, on approved credit'. For example, a car maker might be running a 'zero per cent financing' campaign in order to sell more vehicles. You might then see '0% APR OAC' in the advertisement. The two pieces are important to understand. The 'APR' means that whatever interest rate you see is the 'annual' interest rate, expressed as a percentage. The second piece is important to discuss since 'on approved credit' means that not everyone will qualify for that promotional (or teaser) rate. If your credit score and your employment history are strong, then you just might qualify for the teaser rate. Not everyone will. That might seem unfair, especially if you don't get offered the rate as seen in the advertisement. Recall, though, that lenders are very, very good at managing risk. Offering loans to those who are financially strong presents less of a risk to a lender, so those loan applications will be viewed favourably; lower interest rates will be offered. The opposite is also true. Not everyone gets the best loan rates as advertised.

Credit cards that pay you!

Credit cards can be used very effectively; they can also inflict maximum financial damage if you are not disciplined.

Use your credit card for virtually all your purchases – bet you didn't see that coming!

Seek out a 'no annual fee cash back credit card' that rewards you in cash. Typically, these cards have reward levels in the 1% to 2% range on several spending categories that you can select. You are going to set up an autopay for this card so that you pay off the entire balance automatically each and every month. You are going to check your bill each month to ensure the transactions are legitimate. Make sure you have enough cash in your bank account for the payment to come out, while still keeping your bank account balance above the minimum balance threshold so as to avoid triggering service charges. Using your credit card to do most of your monthly spending means that you will carry a large balance in your bank account, and then it will be cleared out when the credit card due date arrives. Be cognizant of this.

This system offers many advantages. First of all, you're never going to pay a penny to use your credit card unless you decide to upgrade to one with a fee – more on this in a moment. Secondly, you are going to get paid in cash to use your credit card. If you put $3,000 of spending on your card monthly, that translates to $36,000 annually. At a 1.5% reward level, that is $540 worth of tax-free cash in your pocket each year. Voila – you get paid to use your credit card, and there's no points program rewards to track that might actually alter your spending! Thirdly, this is an excellent way to build your credit score since it demonstrates that you are able to handle credit wisely. This creates a crucial positive track record that will work in your favour when you apply for access to larger amounts of credit (such as a mortgage) and can potentially secure more favourable rates. Fourthly, it builds financial discipline since your goal is to pay off the balance each month, effectively putting in place a system where you live within your means month after month.

Following this system will allow you to take control of your credit card usage!

Penny says...

Carrying a credit card balance from month to month is bad news. Carrying even a modest balance of $2,000 on a card that charges 19.99% annual interest will result in $400 worth of annual interest payments, and you still owe the entire $2,000. Your credit score will take a hit too. A job shock could also leave you exposed to needing to make these interest payments for long periods of time.

Why would you possibly pay a fee for a premium credit card?

Some premium credit cards come with hefty annual fees – think $100 to $200. Why would you possibly pay a fee when 'no fee' options are available? Some of these premium credit cards offer higher reward levels across all spending categories. If you pay a $150 annual fee for a card that pays 2% cash back on all of your spending, and you typically put $3,000 on the card monthly, that equates to $720 in annual rewards cash. When compared to a 1.5% reward level for a no fee card that would generate $540 in cash rewards for that same spending level, the annual $150 fee is worth it.

Premium credit cards also typically come with a wide range of, well, premium features beyond those offered by no fee credit cards. These cards typically offer extended warranty coverage for purchases made using the card. Ever buy an item at a store and pay to extend a warranty at the checkout when asked by the clerk? Put those purchases on a premium credit card and those days are over. Enjoy travelling? Some of these cards wave foreign exchange fees and offer annual airline credits. They also typically offer auto rental insurance coverage, so you can waive the collision damage waiver and loss damage waiver on the rental when you book it online, or at the rental counter. By the way, when you rent an automobile, always bring along that little pink slip that you put in your vehicle's glove box that proves you have auto insurance. The auto rental desk will ask who provides your auto insurance, and having this slip is going to avoid brain freeze at the check-in counter.

As long as I don't go over my credit card limit, I'm in good shape, right? Wrong!

One of the factors that impacts your credit score is called credit utilization. If you are in the habit of using a credit card with a small credit limit, such as $1,500, and you typically charge over $1,000 monthly, your credit score is going to take a hit. Shoot to keep the balance below 30% of the credit limit to strengthen your credit score since your current debt level is highly weighted when it comes to how that score is calculated. Call the credit card company to have your credit limit bumped or get another credit card, but plan on keeping your monthly balance below 30% of each card's credit limit.

Again, using a credit card such that the new balance is above 30% of the credit limit, and then paying off the full balance each month, seems like a good strategy, but it will hurt your credit score. Keep those balances below 30% of your credit limit on a regular basis.

Penny says...

Plan ahead when it comes to needing cash. Avoid the need to do a cash advance using your credit card. For example, finding yourself in a cash crunch at a night club and turning to an automated teller machine to do a credit card cash advance is not ideal. You will pay interest beginning the day of the cash advance, and that interest rate will likely be even higher than the credit card's interest rate on purchases. You will likely be assessed fees - lots of fees - for that cash advance too, and you most definitely will not be earning any reward points for that transaction.

Lines of credit – use them wisely...or else!

Think of a line of credit as being like a big credit card. As a matter of fact, both credit cards and lines of credit are classified as 'revolving credit' because of their similarities in allowing account holders to repeatedly borrow or access credit, up to a set limit.

Lines of credit can be both 'secured' with collateral or 'unsecured'. A home equity line of credit (HELOC) is an example of a secured line of credit where the home acts as the collateral to back up the loan. With a HELOC, you get approved for a certain limit based on your home's value and existing mortgage; you can then draw against that limit at any time. If you have built up a lot of equity in your home, the HELOC limit can be large. There are fees associated with opening a HELOC, but your lender may cover some (or all) of these fees, if asked, because this is a lucrative source of revenue for lenders.

As you'll see in a moment, a HELOC can be dangerous if used carelessly.

Much like with a credit card, you will only pay interest on the amount that you use and only for as long as you have a balance. Many lines of credit require that you make payments monthly that are the greater of i) a modest minimum payment such as $25, or ii) the interest payment on the outstanding balance. You carry the balance of the line of credit as debt, but there's no payment schedule that forces you to pay the outstanding balance back. In that important way, lines of credit are not like a mortgage nor a car loan that have set terms that require you to pay back both principal and interest. Car loans and mortgages have end dates; lines of credit normally do not.

A HELOC can be viewed as a second mortgage behind the existing mortgage on your home; however, the biggest difference is that you aren't required to pay back the outstanding balance on the HELOC using a payment schedule.

Unsecured lines of credit usually have higher interest rates than secured lines of credit because the lender doesn't have any collateral to back the loan. Regardless, lines of credit have interest rates that are significantly below credit card interest rates. The interest rate connected to a line of credit usually 'floats'; the rate will go up and down according to the lender's 'prime rate' – more on this when we look at variable-rate versus fixed-rate mortgages in 'Part VI – Mastering Real Estate'.

Canadians love their lines of credit. We use them heavily. When used properly, they are a powerful personal financial tool. They allow us to access often sizable amounts of money for virtually any purpose, at any time without needing to apply for a loan. Given today's ultralow interest rates, the interest rate payments can be very manageable. The 'interest only' payments are also appealing. For example, a HELOC with a floating interest rate of 'prime + 1%' (the interest rate on a line of credit is usually expressed this way) in a low interest rate environment might require payments of under $300 each month on a $100,000 HELOC balance.

Ponder that for a moment. You could rack up $100,000 worth of spending and then finance it by borrowing at relatively low interest rates, yet only have to pay $300 a month. Do you see how tempting that is? Do you see how that can be a total debt trap? It's all about the cash flow to many, many people, as opposed to being about the actual amount of debt. Get that new car today – you deserve it! Put in on your line of credit! Didn't get a raise this year but want to take the family on that five-figure European vacation or cruise? Put it on the line of credit! Racked up some credit card spending from the holidays and want to get it off your credit card? Put it on the line of credit! (That's actually

Part II: Mastering Debt

a good strategy – it's called debt consolidation – but it still usually comes from a lack of saving and/or a lack of financial understanding and/or a lack of financial discipline.)

What are we using our HELOCs for?

Many Canadians have a HELOC that they don't use or haven't 'tapped'. Many, though, have tapped their HELOC aggressively. In a 2018 Canada Mortgage and Housing Corporation (CMHC) report, it was revealed that the average HELOC balance in the country was just over $60,000. When you factor out those who have a HELOC but have no outstanding balance, you are left with a clearer picture of the debt crisis. The average HELOC amount owing for those Canadians who are carrying a balance is in the $100,000 range.[3]

In a 2019 report, the CMHC published results from a survey of Canadians who have a HELOC. The survey asked, "What did you use your HELOC for? Select all that apply." Here are the responses along with some brief explanations, where needed:

- Renovation 49% (for real estate – e.g., remodelling the kitchen)

- Debt consolidation 22% (combining high interest debts, like credit card balances)

- Purchase a vehicle 19%

- Day-to-day expenses 19%

- Emergency fund 14%

- Vacation/travel 13%

- Residential property 11% (purchasing residential property)

- Financial investments 11% (purchasing investment products)[4]

This leads us to an important question – "Are these examples of 'good debt' or 'bad debt'?"

81

'Good debt' versus 'bad debt' – there is definitely a difference!

Debt is a reality. Paying cash for big ticket items like cars and real estate isn't realistic. You will take on debt. We pay our debts over time with income, so there's another reason to take steps to plan your career path so as to grow your income over the years.

What's the difference between good debt and bad debt? Good debt comes with low interest rates and allows you to improve your financial situation. Bad debt hurts you financially.

What are some examples of good debt? Borrowing money using a mortgage to buy real estate is good debt since real estate tends to go up in value. Borrowing money through a student loan to attend Grad School in a field that is in demand is good debt since you are investing in yourself, and this tends to lead to earnings growth. Borrowing money using a line of credit to complete a home renovation is good debt since maintaining or updating your real estate is a fantastic way to support your property's price appreciation. Borrowing money to buy rental units might make sense for you – more on this in 'Part VI – Mastering Real Estate'.

What does bad debt look like? Using a credit card to pay for an expensive vacation, and then carrying that high interest debt on your credit card for many months is bad debt. Getting a car loan to buy a brand-new car is bad debt because new cars depreciate very quickly, and you could have taken on way less debt by buying a quality used car. Using a line of credit to pay for day-to-day expenses because your lifestyle can't be financed through income is bad debt. Going to a payday loan outlet to borrow $1,000 that you need now because you have to pay some unexpected bills is bad debt. You should have an emergency fund to cover financial challenges like this (as opposed to paying simply outrageous interest costs at the payday loan outlet). By the way, viewing a line of credit as an emergency fund is not wise. You want to dip into savings when an emergency hits, as opposed to taking on more debt.

Bad debt can wreck you financially in very short order. Bad debt can also creep up on you; having the balance on a HELOC grow by $10,000 a year for ten years leaves you with six figures worth of this debt! Avoid taking on bad debt. If you have bad debt such as a credit card balance that you have been carrying for some time now, pay it off as soon as possible and redirect the saved interest payments to your savings!

Good debt can help you prosper financially, if it's managed properly.

However, the best debt is the one that you just paid off. Being debt-free has incredible benefits that include increasing available monthly cash flow and the peace of mind that comes with knowing that you can't be pushed into bankruptcy by your creditors. Remember, creditors push people into bankruptcy as a result of not being able to pay back debts – but people take on all the debt in the first place.

Be cautious when it comes to borrowing to invest. You might feel that dipping into your HELOC to purchase investment products is an example of good debt since hopefully the investment grows in value. This strategy (leveraging) can be profitable, but brings special risks, since you could lose money that isn't even yours. If you invest $20,000 from your HELOC, and the investment falls by 10% in the short term, you will still owe $20,000 (plus interest) but your investment will be worth only $18,000. In this case, you are losing money ($2,000) that isn't even yours. This can quickly cause stress and lead to poor decisions.

Penny says...

Not all debts are created equal. Save, save, save so as to be in a position to only take on debt that is 'good debt'. Taking on loads of 'bad debt' will sabotage your financial life and destroy your ability to reach your financial goals.

How does debt consolidation work?

With life, comes debt. As the years go by, debts that were seemingly small and innocuous can grow. All of a sudden, the monthly interest payments that were once under $100 are now much larger. That may be the time to look at debt consolidation, especially if those small interest payments are coming from credit card debt or payday loan outlet debt or even car loan debt, which may carry interest rates that are comfortably into the double-digit range annually. Consolidating several of these debts and paying them off using a HELOC may save you hundreds of dollars each month in interest payments. Direct those savings to paying down the HELOC balance.

By the way, debt consolidation is an excellent debt management strategy – if you find yourself carrying a lot of high interest debt. Autosaving aggressively and living within your means are the ways to avoid finding yourself in this position.

The time to apply for credit is when you are in strong shape financially!

You've just received the bad news that you have been downsized at work. You knew about the benefits of setting up an emergency fund, but there was always another spending priority – you really don't have any significant level of savings at all. Does this sound like the perfect time to visit your bank's website so as to apply for a new credit card or car loan or mortgage or HELOC? Of course not!

Companies know this. Strong, well-managed companies will often take steps to access additional funding when times are good so that they are not put in jeopardy by needing to apply for this funding when financial challenges hit. For example, Alphabet (the parent of Google) issued $10B worth of corporate debt in 2020 at record low interest rates, while Apple also issued $5.5B of corporate debt that same year. Both of these companies had massive cash balances but chose to access additional credit during favourable times given their sector dominance and record low interest rates.

Penny says...

The time to apply for a credit card or a line of credit is when you are working and are in good shape financially. By the way, if your bank sends you an offer to increase your line of credit or credit card limit, take it - assuming that you have the discipline to control your spending. There may come a time when you are in financial peril and need a line of credit increase or a credit card limit bump. How accommodating is your Big Bank likely to be then?

Payday loan outlets – don't even make them your absolute last, last choice!

Have you ever noticed how many payday loan outlets are scattered in the suburbs across this country? Make a point of looking for them the next time you are out and about.

They are opportunists. They know Canadians are heavily indebted, and they know the right buttons to push. When you see signs touting 'instant loans' or 'quick loans' or 'no paperwork' or 'no credit check', you'll know that you've found a payday loan outlet. The outlets are often found in areas dominated by high-density housing where they are in the plain sight of those who may need short-term cash.

The business model works because the interest rate is exorbitant. Read the small print on the posters at any of these outlets or on their websites to see the full details. You will likely see something like this: "We will charge you $15 per $100 borrowed. On a $500 loan for 14 days, the total cost of borrowing is $75, with a total amount owing of $375 and an APR of 391.07%." That's not a typo.

Don't put yourself in a position where these outlets are your only option to access money. Calling the 'Bank of Mom & Dad' is way better on every level.

What do you mean 'I'm not worthy?' There's more to credit worthiness than just your credit score!

Yes, your credit score is viewed by lenders when you apply for credit. For bigger debt applications such as mortgages, your credit worthiness is assessed using what's known as 'The 5 Cs of Credit'. These 5 Cs – collateral, credit, character, capital and capacity – are used by lenders to do a deeper analysis of your credit worthiness. These factors will be explored later in 'Part VI – Mastering Real Estate'.

Be 'debt-free after your first degree' or diploma!

Massive spending awaits you shortly after you complete your post-secondary years. You will likely get a car, move out, furnish an apartment that you rent and then look to buy real estate. That will be a spending binge that will make your head spin, and it's the reality for countless young adults. You will be on the 'debt train' and you will have lots of company.

In Ontario, 15% of insolvencies involved student debt, with an average of nearly $14,000 in student loans and $45,000 in total unsecured debt.[5]

You will do yourself a huge financial favour if you take steps to graduate with little or no debt from college or university after earning your first degree or diploma! If you are pursuing an apprenticeship, you will likely be earning money as you log hours while moving through your apprenticeship training, so school-related debt should be a moot point for you – bravo!

Can you 'go local'? Is there a post-secondary institute close to your home that offers a program that interests you? If the answer is yes, consider choosing it; living at home saves on housing costs. Sure, you might have a strong desire to move away from home to go to school for many reasons, even if remote learning is an option. You can still experience living in another place by taking summer jobs outside of your home town. Programs with co-operative education components open this door up too, as do programs with internships. The big, big bonus with these programs is that you are immersed in work settings in your field throughout your post-secondary years. What a way to get experience, but also, what a way to make connections that can lead to employment offers when you graduate!

If you are able to commute to school and the distance is reasonable, consider buying a quality used car or using transit as opposed to moving away from home. Hybrid remote learning options and the ability to tailor-make school schedules might make it easy for you to limit your physical trips to school on a weekly basis, too.

Seek out and apply for grants, scholarships and bursaries. These are not loans; they are sources of money to fund your schooling costs that don't have to be repaid.

Don't plan on taking on significant hours of part-time work while you are taking classes. Invariably, the school pressures will hit when you have shifts at work, and that's a formula for getting worn out, getting sick and blowing high-stakes exams. Failing out is common. Don't let money be the root cause of this for you.

Your first degree is important but, for many, subsequent training, certificates, and post-graduate work are coming and, with them, come major costs too. Take steps to graduate debt-free after your first degree or diploma.

And then go one better!

Live at home with your parents for your first year of full-time work after finishing school. Doesn't that sound fun! Well, here's the deal. Tell your parents that if they are open to letting you live at home for your first year of full-time work, you will endeavour to save virtually your entire year's income. Yes, you can celebrate with your friends and go on a vacation – but not a two-month European vacation. Yes, you can get a car – but not an expensive one and not a new one (more on this in 'Part V – Mastering Your Ride'). Imagine how far those savings will go to helping you accumulate a good chunk of the down payment on your first real estate purchase! Now that probably sounds a bit more fun, doesn't it!

If you are in a relationship, see if your partner can do this too. You will fast track your financial life more than you can imagine and create a savings mindset that will last a lifetime. Taking steps to have a significant real estate down payment in your pocket, only one short year after graduating debt-free, will set you up for financial success on so many levels.

Key takeaways from 'Mastering Debt'

→ realize the importance of interest rates when it comes to the cost of debt

→ have an awareness of the role that collateral plays in the lending process

→ be aware of the importance of your credit score

→ understand the steps that you can take to improve your credit score

→ use a credit card in such a way that it pays you

→ understand the dangers and benefits of using lines of credit, including HELOCs

→ know that there is both 'good debt' and 'bad debt'

→ take action to avoid 'bad debt'

→ realize that the best time to apply for credit is when you're in good shape financially

→ take steps to graduate with little or no debt after completing your first degree or diploma

Part III

Mastering Investing

In 'Mastering Investing', we'll cover the basics of how to go about investing. Consider the content to be like an 'Investing 101' course. During my teaching days, my students would tell me that they knew that they had to save, but they had no idea how to invest. Perhaps you feel the same way. You likely haven't learned much about investing in school. The terminology – bull market, bear market, correction, etc. – can be intimidating, while the idea of losing your money can be very scary. The sheer number of investment choices makes it difficult for many to get started on their investing journey. It's crucial not to be overwhelmed, though. We must invest to grow our wealth, and achieve our long-term financial goals.

Crucial lessons in this part of the book include the 'get rich SLOW' approach to investing, using index products to buy the entire stock market as opposed to picking stocks, risk tolerance, and the importance of keeping fees low.

There is no financial independence without investing. The key lessons found here will allow you to invest with confidence.

Get rich SLOW!

Recall that a key, actionable component of the 'earn, save, invest cycle' revolves around setting up and funding different savings buckets or accounts for different future financial needs. You often can see these costs coming, so saving for them is a given if you want to thrive financially. For example, you are very likely going to need money down the road for costs such as retirement, a down payment on a first or next home, a first or next car, post-secondary school for the kids (if that's applicable) and to have cash in an emergency fund. You can see these costs coming, so set up a savings bucket for each of them now.

You will fund these accounts the day after you are paid (autosave) by moving the money out of your main bank account and 'hiding' the money on yourself. Transferring the money to a virtual bank works well here since the cash is 'out of sight', and you are easily able to open multiple small accounts that can be named after the savings goals. Small amounts are fine, especially when you are just beginning to fund the savings buckets through autosaving.

There's nothing wrong with 'only' transferring $50 into each account every two weeks to get you going. At least you've started!

This 'get rich slow' approach is measured and it works – you just stick to your plan. In this way, it is straightforward and simple to understand, but it's difficult for many to action this over the long term. The reason why many struggle is that the process requires discipline; you need to follow the plan for many years and grow the amount that you deposit as your income grows.

It's also very important to understand that there are really only three key variables involved when it comes to amassing a large financial nest egg for a significant long-term goal such as your retirement fund. Those variables are:

1. The MONEY that you save and invest

2. The RATE OF RETURN that you earn on those investments

3. The TIME that you to let that money grow

With the 'get rich slow' approach, you leverage the most powerful variable – time – but the only way to take advantage of the power of time is to start sooner than later. Start now.

All right, the autosave is working. How do I invest the money in each bucket?

To answer this, you must consider two key variables – time and your risk appetite. We'll look at time first and your risk appetite in a little bit.

You must consider time. Categorize your saving buckets into timeframes using this model:

- Short-term – up to three years

- Medium-term – 3 to 10 years

- Long-term – beyond 10 years

  Simple.

Help me with 'short-term', please!

Short-term costs are the ones that you expect to pay on a regular basis. Cash that is saved for these goals should be accessible and safe. These costs tend to repeat and are often based on our personal preferences. They are the costs that we see coming in the next thirty-six months. They are definitely not going to be long-term in nature. Here's a sample listing:

- emergency fund (priority one and definitely needs its own account)

- gifts – birthday, holiday, anniversary, etc. (again, these will be spent on experiences as opposed to stuff)

- vacations (be sure to save for these since they are 'memory makers'!)

- property repairs (estimate at 1% of market value of property – more on this in 'Part VI – Mastering Real Estate')

- car repairs

The money that gets saved and deposited into these savings buckets can be left right in the savings accounts. Ideally, these accounts will be 'high-interest savings accounts' – virtual banks or credit unions are good choices here – but the reality is that the interest rates are so low on bank accounts nowadays that the interest earned will be immaterial. The accounts should really be named 'barely better than nothing savings accounts'.

You can look at short-term guaranteed investment certificates (GICs) options for short-term goals too. These GICs will earn a marginally higher interest rate, but your money is locked up for the duration of the GIC term so you want to keep that term short to match your short-term timeline need for the cash.

You could choose a GIC ladder here. This involves having your short-term cash structured in several different GICs, all of which have various maturity dates (due dates). For example, you might have your short-term funds structured in this way:

- 40% in a high-interest saving account

- 20% in a cashable GIC (which typically can be cashed at anytime but interest earned will be forfeited if cashed within a set number of days – usually 90 days)

- 20% in a one-year GIC (that matures in one year)

- 20% in a three-year GIC

You may want to approach a deposit broker to set up and manage this piece on your behalf, once the dollar amounts in your short-term savings account are large enough that the interest earned becomes material to you.

The interest earned on these accounts will be low – because interest rates are so low – for these short-term savings buckets, but remember you need the money sooner than later, so accepting a smaller return is just fine given that you can't afford to have the balances fluctuate. You are going to need these dollars to be there when you need to access the money in the short term. In financial circles, the goal here is called 'capital preservation' since you are taking steps to protect your dollars as opposed to growing them.

Simple.

Your deposits are insured within limits

The federal government protects deposits that are housed at member financial institutions to the tune of up to $100,000 per account through the Canadian Deposit and Insurance Corporation (CDIC). GICs, savings and chequing accounts, and foreign currency accounts are all covered, whereas mutual funds and stocks are not. You can have deposits in multiple accounts (e.g., joint and individual) and at multiple institutes to protect more of your dollars.[1]

For example, you could open a chequing account with a member financial institution such as one of our Big Banks, and that account would have up to $100,000 worth of CDIC coverage. Then, opening a joint savings account would provide an additional $100,000 of CDIC coverage. Opening a Tax-Free Savings Account (TFSA) would add more deposit insurance, as would opening a Registered Retirement Savings Plan (RRSP). You could then do that all over again at another member institution, and the coverage limits would be available to you again.

Deposit brokers are, of course, aware of these coverages and can provide valuable assistance.

Remember, CDIC coverage protects deposits; stocks and mutual funds are not included.

Penny says...

For credit union members, provincial regulations provide protection on insurable deposits. For example, the Credit Union Deposit Insurance Corporation of British Columbia (CUDICBC) provides 100% coverage on insurable deposits for members of BC credit unions.[2] For those in Ontario who are credit union members, the Financial Services Regulatory Authority of Ontario (FSRA) protects insurable deposits of up to $250,000 in non-registered accounts and unlimited coverage is provided for insurable deposits in registered accounts such as a TFSA.[3]

Now, help me with 'medium-term' and 'long-term' too, please!

Medium-term is the label we use for our savings buckets that contain cash we believe we will need in the three to ten-year timeframe. Long-term goals stretch out beyond a decade.

Medium-term goals might include:

- down payment for a car

- down payment for real estate

- tuition for continuing education

Long-term goals might include:

- upsizing real estate

- kids' education costs

- retirement

For these goals, it's time to do some investing, specifically investing in the stock market so as to grow our money. The cool thing is that you don't have to know anything about individual stocks to successfully invest in the stock market, if you know what to buy.

We have to do some learning first, though!

Time to talk about risk tolerance!

Now that we understand the importance of timeframes when it comes time to investing, let's consider risk tolerance. When it comes to investing, a good way of defining risk is the chance that you will lose your money. Investment risk can be mitigated or managed.

We manage or mitigate risk in virtually every part of our lives. Consider…

- Did you put on your seatbelt the last time you got in a car to manage the risk of getting injured or getting a ticket for driving without using a seatbelt?

- Did you wear any equipment when you last took part in sports activities to take safety precautions?

- Did you make sure that your car insurance is in place in order to manage the financial risk of having a car accident?

Why, then, are we so afraid of embracing investment risk when it too can be managed, especially over the long term? Again, risk can be managed.

If you know that you would not be able to sleep at night if your investments fall by 10%, that's important to understand because stocks do go up and down in value. If you can't tolerate a market dip, then your tolerance is such that investing in the stock market may not be suitable for you. That may mean that you will have to save more because your savings won't be growing very quickly, given today's ultralow interest rates. Remember, savers love high interest rates, and today's low interest rates cause problems for savers because the investments just don't grow very quickly, unfortunately.

I don't even understand what the stock market is ☺

You can buy pieces (known as shares) of companies. Those companies' shares trade on stock exchanges. These pieces give you ownership of a small slice of the business. For this reason, shares are often called equities since they represent ownership. These businesses are public corporations – they are owned by shareholders and have shares that trade on stock markets. There are both preferred and common shares. For our purposes, when corporate 'shares' are mentioned, we are talking about common shares since common share values are driven by, and move in tandem with, corporate profitability in the long term. Preferred shares are different, and will be discussed soon when we consider bonds.

When we hear it reported that the stock markets are up 20% this year, what that means is the stock index for that market is up 20%. Think of the index as a class average. Your report card in school might have indicated that the final class average in your math course was 72%, but your final mark was 75%. You would be pleased to learn that you beat the class average or 'index'. Investors often compare their results to these index 'benchmarks' to judge performance.

What drives stock market results or stock market indices over the long term? The simplest answer is corporate profits. If the profits of the corporations in the stock market are rising over time, investors will want to pay more to buy pieces of those companies. They will bid up the prices of these corporate shares, and the stock market will rise. Again, remember that when we hear that the stock market is up, that really means that the stock market index for that market is up. Increased corporate profitability drives up stock market indices over the long term. The opposite is true too.

I heard the DOW is up a thousand points for the year. What does that mean?

The United States has some major stock indices that are important to understand.

• Dow Jones Industrial Average – commonly called 'The Dow Jones'

     o Viewed as the 'granddaddy of them all' since it is a very old index o Contains 30 of the largest US companies – examples include Walmart, Disney, Intel, McDonald's and Nike

- Massive, global companies

- S&P 500 – commonly called 'The S&P'

  o Same idea as the The Dow Jones but now we have about 500 of the biggest US companies

    - There are often a few more than 500 for a number of reasons

  o Therefore, we have a broader index

  o The 11 US market sectors are well-represented

    - Examples of these sectors include technology, healthcare, real estate and financials

- NASDAQ Composite Index – commonly called 'The NASDAQ'

  o The major US tech companies are in this index

    - Companies include tech giants such as Microsoft, Amazon, Apple, Meta (Facebook's revised company name) and Alphabet (Google's parent company)

All of these indices had varied start dates, and have current index valuations that also widely differ. As a result, the fact that an index might be up 1,000 points is not as meaningful as knowing the percentage gains or losses.

If you look at all the companies on the entire planet, the US companies dominate.

If you wanted to buy an entire corporation, you could theoretically do that. You would need to buy all of the shares of that company that are publicly traded on the stock market. That dollar amount is called market capitalization, and the amounts are big; that's an understatement.

In 2020, Apple became the first US company to pass \$2T in market capitalization.

Do you remember my counting exercise from earlier? Let's try it again. Begin counting. Keep counting and do nothing else; no sleeping and no eating. Count one number per second and keep that up. You would be able to count to 86,400 in one day. Want to guess how long it would take you to get to two trillion, which can also be written as 2,000,000,000,000?

It would take you over 63,000 YEARS.

These are big companies. US companies dominate the list of the world's largest companies when measured by market capitalization. These behemoths are all household names and are 'category killers' who dominate their respective market sectors – think Apple, Microsoft, Amazon.

As a matter of fact, if you add up the market capitalization (stock market valuations) of all the shares traded on stock markets on the planet, US companies would total well over 50% of global stock market capitalization. The point is that we must be invested in US companies to have access to these category killer companies.

Another major global index is the MSCI EAFE, which covers Europe, Australasia and the Far East. MSCI stands for Morgan Stanley Capital International, and this index is commonly referred to as the EAFE. It contains shares of companies from major developed markets outside of North America. Major countries represented in this index include Japan, Germany and the United Kingdom. The MSCI EAFE index consists of companies that represent over 30% of global stock market capitalization.

What about Canada?

What about Canada's major index? It's called the S&P/TSX Composite Index, and it's commonly referred to as the TSX for Toronto Stock Exchange. It contains approximately 230 of Canada's largest, most-recognizable corporations. All of our Big Banks are included. Other major companies in the index include Shopify, Enbridge, Brookfield Asset Management, Canadian National Railway, Canadian Pacific Railway, TC Energy, Thomson Reuters and Bell Canada, to name just a few.

Note that Canada's market capitalization as a percentage of world stock market is extremely small – well under 5%.

Also, note that Canada's stock market index is light on both 'tech' and 'healthcare' companies; you definitely want to be invested in these sectors in the long-term. As you would expect, this lack of exposure to tech and healthcare stocks has led to the S&P/TSX Composite Index's chronic underperformance, when compared to the major US stock market indices.

The only logical conclusion is that having your investment dollars tied to only Canadian companies is going to stop you from being exposed to massive, category killer companies (like Amazon) in tech and healthcare that you clearly want to own as an investor in the long term.

You're going to see lots of references to the major, broad-based US index – S&P 500 – going forward in this book, and now you know why! Keeping too much money invested in Canadian equities is just plain foolish.

Penny says...

Oh no, Canada! Be sure your investments travel the planet. Having all your money invested in Canadian companies has been a guaranteed way to underperform the global indices in the past, given our limited exposure to the tech sector and the healthcare sector. For example, the annualized ten-year total return for the S&P/TSX Composite Index through the end of May 2021 was 6.81% in Canadian dollars[4] versus an annualized ten-year total return for the S&P 500 over the same period of 14.38% in US dollars.[5] Ouch!

Here's a 'crash' course in stock market terms

Stock markets can move violently at times. Periods of relative quiet where the stock market 'trades sideways' (doesn't move much in either direction) can quickly come to an end. Sometimes this is caused by 'news' such as surprising economic data indicating that the economy might be unexpectedly slowing down or picking up. Sometimes it is caused by investor fear and greed; FOMO (fear of missing out) is alive and well when viewing the stock market too. When the markets start moving violently up or down, this is called market volatility.

When markets are moving up dramatically, investors see their portfolios going up in value. The opposite is true when markets plunge. There are some terms to describe these market movements.

- Bull market – bulls charge ahead so, when the market is up by at least 20%, that's called a bull market

- Bear market - bears can maul you so, when the market is down by at least 20%, that's called a bear market

- Market crash – synonymous with bear markets

- Market correction – when markets drop by at least 10%

Why would anyone invest in stocks if they might fall?

The reason why we are willing to tolerate our investments falling or being volatile in the short term is that, over the long term, stock markets go up in value.

This is really the key piece. Over the long term, stock markets rise.

These gains are not linear and are not predictable in the short term. Periods of negative returns (your portfolio falling in value) are definitely a possibility. However, when the time horizon is long enough (think 10+ years), there's a very, very high probability that a broad-based stock index will generate healthy, positive returns.

Stock valuations go up over time because profits grow. When a company's earnings become very strong and the prospects look bright, the corporate leadership group (think senior management and the board of directors) often reward shareholders by 'dividing up' some of the profits in the form of cash dividends and giving them to shareholders. Strong, powerful companies take great pride in raising dividends yearly. This, too, acts to increase share prices because there is an expectation of rising dividend payouts for investors. These dividend payments are reflected in share prices and are included in stock market index results. Large, strong companies that have stable or increasing dividends are often referred to as 'large cap' companies (short for 'large capitalization') or 'Blue Chip' companies. By the way, all of these companies grew to be big companies which means that many small companies (called 'small caps') will also grow to be superb companies down the road. Remember that Microsoft was very small, back in the day.

Over the very long term, major broad-based stock market indices have performed extremely well because they are filled with many Blue Chip companies. For example, the S&P 500 index returned a compounded annual gain of 10.2% from 1965 to 2020 when dividends are included, based on a table from Berkshire Hathaway Inc.'s 2020 Annual Report.[6] Interestingly enough, Berkshire Hathaway's shares returned a compounded annual gain of 20.0% over this same period, as shown in that table. Warren Buffett is the Chairman and Chief Executive Officer (CEO) of this company, and he is viewed as one of the finest investors on the planet; his company's results speak for themselves.

Remember that these results are not linear. When looking at results from 1965 forward (as per that table in Berkshire Hathaway's 2020 Annual Report), the S&P 500's best annual percentage change was +37.6% in 1995. The worst loss was -37.0% in 2008 when the Great Recession and financial crisis rocked the world's economies.

There will be years of superb gains (think 30%+) and periods of weakness (think of losses of 30%+) if past performance is any indication of future performance. This is what volatility looks like. Fees paid by individual investors must also be considered as a drag on performance.

What are the chances of losing money when investing in a broad-based stock market index? Past results can provide valuable insights here. Let's examine the Canadian stock market's long-term performance (dating back to the mid-1950s) as measured by the S&P/TSX Composite Total Return Index. You can ascertain the likelihood that the index was up in value over various timeframes by backtesting. Over any one-year period, the index was higher in value (compared to the previous year) 73% of the time. That rose to 83% over two years. However, once you stretch that out to any five-year period, the results are reassuring; the index was up 98% of the time. Past results aren't a guarantee of future results, but they help us manage expectations.[7]

Penny says...

Stock market crashes get headlines but the markets recover these losses, and march forward. The reality is that stocks go up in value over the long term. Thinking otherwise flies in the face of stock market performance dating back decades and decades.

You don't need to be a 'stock picker' to invest in the stock market! There's a better, easier way!

Of critical importance is to understand that you don't need to select any specific companies at all to invest in stocks. You can just invest in the indices! You can buy parts (known as 'units') of an 'index fund' that buys an index or a number of indices.

This is a wonderful option since you are literally able to buy pieces of all of the world's major companies and, since great companies don't shrink themselves to greatness, we want to own all of these major category killer companies.

This is also known as passive investing since you are just 'buying the index', as opposed to buying a product where a manager 'picks stocks' in order to attempt to beat the index.

Best of all, you can even 'buy the entire world' by buying units of a global index fund!

Penny says...

Too intimidated to pick stocks? Forget about it and 'buy the world' by buying units of a simple global index fund that gives you access to major indices around the planet. It really is that simple!

Index investing is so powerful because...

Why is index investing such a powerful strategy? It allows us to manage investment risk in an economical way! How?

- DIVERSIFICATION!

    o Think of the phrase 'you don't want all of your eggs in one basket!' and you will understand diversification

    o Diversify by...

    - Company

    - Sector

    - Size of company

    - Geography

    - Market maturity (developed and developing markets/ emerging markets)

We can smooth out stock market ups and downs by using diversification!

Also, of note is that companies often have life cycles and can dominate, but then fall away or get replaced as leaders (think of Nortel or Sears). Market indices are, however, updated regularly so that great companies are added and laggards are dropped. This is crucial since it allows you to 'buy and hold' a broad index fund for long, long periods without worrying too much about the holdings becoming filled with weak companies. The strong companies that are coming up 'grow' their way into these indices. In a sense, strong companies are added, and weak companies are removed. The custodians of the stock market indices do these reviews on a regular basis. Therefore, these major broad indices contain companies you want included because we know that, in the long term, growing corporate profitability drives positive stock market index performance.

Penny says...

Diversification is one of the absolute key strategies when it comes to investing success. Passive index investing is built on diversification. The opposite of diversification is concentration – by company, sector, size, etc. – and with concentration comes increased risk. Mitigate the risk by diversifying – embrace passive index investing!

LOW FEES! Fees matter – they really matter!

You can buy an index product that replicates a major stock index (also known as an equity index product) that comes with annual fees (expressed as the management expense ratio or MER) in the .20 of 1% range (or .20%). Compare this with paying an experienced manager to 'select' stocks where you will be charged a MER in the 2.25% range for an equity mutual fund (a fund managed by a professional manager who selects stocks on behalf of fund unit holders).

This is an incredible difference in fees. Think of it this way…2% 2% 2% 2% 2% 2% 2% for decades. It adds up. These fees can easily eat one-third of your investment portfolio compared with just buying index products.

Perhaps you've seen those unsettling robo-advisor commercials where the client challenges the investment advisor because the fees are eating up 30% of the portfolio. That's what that advertising campaign is designed to highlight. Keeping investment fees low is so, so important.

But surely the higher fees are worth it because those professional money managers must all beat the index!

Think again!

Over the long term, professional money managers struggle mightily to beat the index. In Canada, where we have some of the highest fees for mutual funds on the planet[8], a small fraction of actively managed equity mutual funds outperforms the index over time frames longer than 10 years.[9]

Buying these actively managed equity mutual funds, then, is choosing to overpay for underperformance.

The lesson? Buy index products that represent the entire world for your long-term investing goals!

Penny says...

Buying actively managed equity mutual funds with a 'star' professional money manager at the helm and paying expensive fees each year is silly. You are paying more for underperformance. They can't routinely beat the index!

Surely a professional money manager will beat the index when the markets crash, right?

You would think so. After all, a professional money manager who manages an equity fund should be able to really add value in the midst of a volatile period where stocks are moving up and down rapidly. During these periods, their 'stock picking' expertise should shine through.

The data says otherwise. The year 2020 was a prime example of a wildly volatile trading period with a rapid market crash after the pandemic began, followed by a rally throughout the rest of the year. How did Canadian equity mutual fund results in 2020 compare with their benchmarks or major indices? The vast, vast majority of Canadian equity mutual funds – 88% – underperformed their benchmark in 2020. Was that a fluke? It should come as no surprise that those results are in line with the previous ten-year average of 84%.[10] Our friends south of the border have experienced the same results; US large cap funds have underperformed the benchmark for eleven consecutive years.[11] This is all just further proof that index investing is an excellent strategy to embrace!

Time to learn how to build an investment portfolio!

Investment portfolios typically have three components – cash, bonds and equities. Adjusting the weighting of these three components in a portfolio is a way of managing risk. We, therefore, need to learn about this.

First, let's make sure we understand the three components.

'Cash' is, well, cash. As discussed earlier, this is money that is safe but won't earn much in interest since it is in a 'high-interest savings account' or GIC. This money is 'liquid' – it's not tied up for long periods of time, and you can access it in short order.

It was noted earlier that companies can issue debt as a way of financing their operations. This long-term company debt is typically issued as bonds. Just as you can buy a corporation's shares on the stock market so, too, can you buy a corporation's bonds on the bond market. Governments issue massive debt too. This is how all those deficit budgets get funded. When you buy a corporate or government bond, you will be paid interest. The interest rates paid by bonds vary depending on how much risk is attached to the bonds and how long you have to hold the bonds before they mature and the money is paid back. Generally speaking, bonds pay a higher interest rate than 'cash' but, given today's ultralow rate environment, bond interest rates are low too.

As discussed, when you buy a corporation's shares or units of an equity index fund or equity mutual fund, you are buying a small piece of ownership in a company or companies. Buying bonds is quite different because you are buying those entities' debts.

There's a danger in holding just cash – it's called inflation!

You might be thinking that investing only in cash is the way to go. There's seemingly no risk since the value doesn't go up or down, and you can get at it when you want – it's liquid.

Unfortunately, cash will actually lose value over time. That needs some explanation.

Let's assume that your parents inherited some money around the time you were born, and they decided to set some of that money aside in a safety deposit box at the bank to pay for your post-secondary education costs, twenty years down the road. They might have set aside $20,000 because that would have nicely covered the cost of four years of a university or college education back then, even if you moved away from home. If they pulled that cash out of the safety deposit box just before you headed off to university or college, they would have realized what inflation does over time. Inflation eats purchasing power. That $20,000 would no longer cover your post-secondary education costs.

We deal with inflation when it comes to thinking about getting a raise at work. If inflation is running at 1% annually in the country, we need to get a raise of 1% just to maintain our purchasing power.

Central banks often set inflation-control targets. The Bank of Canada inflation-control target is 2% in the medium term which is the mid-point of the target range of 1% to 3%. Inflation in Canada has been very tame. It's been decades since it was above 5% on a year-over-year annual basis.

The 'real rate of return' of an investment is the return less the inflation rate. Cash accounts pay virtually nothing nowadays and, even with muted inflation, holding cash will lead to a decrease in purchasing power over time. This is almost always the case – it's quite normal for the inflation rate to be above the interest rate that our Big Banks pay on savings accounts.

As an aside, you may have heard that central banks in some countries have turned to 'negative interest rates' as a way to stimulate their economies. In this case, the bank will deduct money from your savings account each month as opposed to paying you interest. This obviously acts as an incentive for consumers to spend as opposed to save. This stimulates the economy and is really a signal that the country is in the throes of an economic crisis. Negative rates are not normal and are not a sign of economic strength.

What about bonds then? What if I just hold bonds?

Recall that bonds represent the debt that companies or governments issue to fund their activities. Investors can 'buy' this debt. We can buy bonds on the bond market but that is usually a practice reserved for 'institutional investors'. These are the big players – think huge pension fund managers – who professionally manage money for others. The rest of us are called 'retail investors' because we manage our own money in our own portfolios.

We – the retail investors – normally acquire bonds through buying units of a bond mutual fund that is actively managed or units of a bond index fund that is passively managed and tracks one of many bond indices.

Bonds pay interest, but their value can also fluctuate due to changes in interest rates. Bond interest rates are usually set or fixed, and for that reason, bonds are also often referred to as 'fixed income'. There is an important relationship at work when it comes to the way that the bond market values bonds. As interest rates rise, bonds go down in value. As interest rates fall, bonds go up in value. A bond from several years ago with a generous fixed rate would be in demand during a time of historically low interest rates; its value would go up. Conversely, a bond issued in the midst of a financial crisis with an extremely low fixed rate will not be as appealing in future years if interest rates move upwards; its value would go down.

Earlier, we noted that a company normally has the right to issue both common stock and preferred stock. As noted, when 'stock' appears in this book, we are discussing common stock. Why? In an odd nuance, preferred shares have very different features than common stock and behave more like bonds than common stocks since preferred shares typically pay a set dividend. As such, preferred shares are quite similar to bonds in that preferred shares tend to move inversely with interest rate changes in the economy. That's the last reference to preferred shares you will see in this book since it is virtually immaterial for our purposes (but it was worth mentioning since you may have heard the term before).

When interest rates are at ultralow levels, they do not have much more room to drop, unless you consider negative interest rates as likely on an ongoing basis. Note that this would be atypical.

As a result, the long-term performance prospects for bonds are muted when interest rates are low. The following chart is worth considering given this backdrop.

CANADA, LONG-TERM INTEREST RATES, 10-YEAR BOND YIELD[12]

(Total, % by annum, monthly, January 1955 – May 2021)

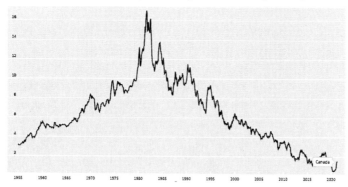

Bonds may, in fact, not return much more than cash does going forward for many years.

In his Chairman's Letter found inside the Berkshire Hathaway Inc. 2020 Annual Report, Warren Buffett writes this: "Fixed-income investors worldwide – whether pension funds, insurance companies or retirees – face a bleak future."[13]

Penny says...

Bonds have just finished moving through almost four decades of outstanding returns. Why? Interest rates slid from double-digit levels to virtually zero from the early 1980s until 2021. Bonds are not well positioned to continue these stellar returns given an ultralow interest rate environment.

Why then hold bonds at all?

We hold bonds because portfolios that are 'all equity' expose the investor to maximum volatility. When volatility hits the stock market, stocks move violently. When they fall far enough, the media picks it up and blasts out unsettling headlines. Nervous investors sell. If your portfolio contains bonds, it won't go down as much when (not 'if') the next stock market crash hits. This makes you less likely to panic and sell. Yes, you likely won't see your portfolio go up as much if you hold bonds, but what good is an 'all equity' portfolio if it opens up the possibility that you panic and sell your equities during a bear market?

We hold bonds to help us weather stock market storms. We hold bonds so that we are less likely to panic and sell our equities when a stock market crash arrives. We hold bonds because stock market crashes can make us irrational. Fear can easily take over. Fear does as much damage as greed when it comes to investment mistakes. We hold bonds to protect ourselves…from ourselves.

Embracing equities – pretty appealing given the ultralow returns elsewhere, even when bears come along for the ride!

Retail investors can own the equity of companies in several ways. They can own stocks directly or through an equity index fund or equity mutual fund.

As discussed, this can be volatile in the short term. Major market crashes have occurred three times in the last quarter century alone – the Dot.com Bust in 1999 and 2000, the Great Recession that accompanied the financial crisis in 2008 and 2009 and the pandemic-fueled crash of 2020.

These crashes were the real thing. The S&P 500 shed 49%, 57% and 34%, respectively, during each of those stock market crashes. In all cases, the S&P 500 went on to recover those losses and hit new highs. With the Dot.com Bust and the Great Recession, the S&P 500 took some time to go on to hit new highs – 31 months and 17 months, respectively.[14] The 2020 pandemic-fueled crash featured a lightening-quick recovery for the S&P 500 that took less than six months for the index to once again post new highs.[15]

Bear markets have tended to vary in length, but the markets recover from them. That's a fact.

Recall that the S&P 500's average annualized return including dividends from 1965 to 2020 was 10.2%. We know that there have been three severe market crashes in just the last two decades, though. How did the markets fair then over these last 20 years? You would think that the results must be far worse given the market carnage that took place when bear markets mauled investor portfolios on three separate occasions during the last twenty years. However, from 2000 to 2020, the S&P 500 averaged an annual return (including dividends) of approximately 7%. That's not too bad at all despite all the negative news around the crashes.[16]

To help with visualizing the S&P 500 performance over the last two-plus decades, here's a chart of that index which clearly shows the market crashes and market recoveries over those years.

S&P 500 PERFORMANCE
(Total, monthly averages of daily closing values, monthly, Jan. 1999 — Sept. 2021)[17]

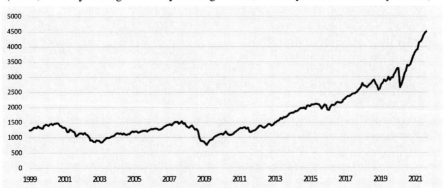

What does Warren Buffett say about stock market returns going forward? In his Chairman's Letter found inside the Berkshire Hathaway Inc. 2019 Annual Report, Buffett writes this:

"What we *can* say is that *if* something close to current rates should prevail over the coming decades and *if* corporate tax rates also remain near the low level businesses now enjoy, it is almost certain that equities will *over time* perform far better than long-term, fixed-rate debt instruments.

That rosy prediction comes with a warning: *Anything* can happen to stock prices tomorrow. Occasionally, there will be major drops in the market, perhaps of 50% magnitude or even greater. But the combination of The American Tailwind, about which I wrote last year, and the compounding wonders described by Mr. Smith, will make equities the much better long-term choice for the individual who does not use borrowed money and who can control his or her emotions. Others? Beware!"[18]

Penny says...

When it comes to evaluating potential investment returns going forward, Buffett predicts that the outlook for bonds is muted. Low interest rates mean cash will earn a very low return too. Embracing equities for long-term investment dollars is a must given this backdrop; think TINA – there is no alternative.

What drives the stock market in the short term does not drive it in the long term

We know that over the long term, broad-based stock market indices rise. We also know that there can be extreme volatility in the short term. Both of these situations are likely to persist. Why?

In the short term, the market moves quickly to digest new information and 'price it in' to value and re-calibrate an individual stock's future expected profitability. A shock like the 9/11 terrorist attack will cause markets to sell off. Bad economic news (think record unemployment at the start of the global pandemic) will cause sell-offs too. A company's quarterly results that exceed analyst expectations (called 'beating the street') will move a company's stock price up quickly. These factors can be 'macro' (broader themed) or 'micro' (company or sector-specific developments) and are often driven by 'fundamentals' which include measurements such as rising sales volumes or rising profits.

A 'herd mentality' definitely thrives, too, when it comes to how we humans invest in the stock market. Investors are driven by their emotions; fear and greed are often driving the bus. These two factors can be powerful market movers as human emotion kicks in during times of euphoria (e.g., FOMO-driven buying during a bull market) or panic (e.g., selling that locks in losses during a violent market crash). In the short term, market volatility is the end result of these forces being unleashed on the market. Markets don't like uncertainty because markets are forward-pricing machines, and uncertainty – think a closely-contested upcoming US presidential election where the candidates are on opposite sides of major policy stances – makes pricing difficult.

That's pretty unpredictable. That is a challenging environment for retail investors.

The good news is that this scenario does not rear its ugly head when we look at long-term stock market performance.

In the long term, clear patterns appear which allows stock markets to accurately price in correct valuations. Years of financial results are analyzed. Weak companies falter and disappear. Strong companies emerge and dominate. In the long term, stock markets are very effective at pricing stocks properly because, with time, what is unknown becomes known.

Again, make no mistake that in the short term, this is anything but an exact science. But in the long term, markets get it right.

Over the long term, volatility gets smoothed out as crashes from the past become blips on charts.

Over the long term, the stock market moves up because the economy keeps growing, and companies prosper financially in this environment.

Getting the correct asset mix inside your long-term portfolio is crucial

The percentage of cash, bonds and equities in any investment account or portfolio will add up to 100%. For long-term goals, your equity weighting should approximate '100% minus your age', assuming that you have a reasonable tolerance for investment risk.

Let's look at two investors: an 80-year-old Nana and her 25-year-old Granddaughter. For our 80-year-old Nana, she should have 100% - 80 years of age = 20% in equities, with the rest in bonds and cash. For Nana's 25-year-old Granddaughter who's beginning to save for retirement, she should have 100% - 25 years of age = 75% in equities, with the rest in bonds and cash.

Why? Nana has less time to recover from a dip in the stock market and so she should not be taking on undue risk. Thus, her equity weighting is small (20%), whereas her Granddaughter has decades until retirement and can, therefore, ride out market volatility.

Penny says...

Some are calling for long-term equity weighting percentages to be bumped closer to '120% minus age' which implies embracing a higher equity weighting. Primary reasons for this include longer life expectancies and muted future bond return expectations. Regardless, the lesson here is that your portfolio risk profile (i.e., equity weighting) will fall as you age, assuming a reasonable risk tolerance.

The 'Rule of 72' and you!

Recall that we learned that there are only three variables involved in amassing a large financial nest egg for a major long-term financial goal such as funding retirement:

1. Money saved and invested

2. The rate of return earned

3. The time that we have that money invested

The 'Rule of 72' provides tremendous insight on the impact of rate of return.

Here's the concept: take 72 and divide it by any rate of return. This will approximate how many years it will take that money to double in value, ignoring inflation.

This means that a high-interest savings account with a beginning balance of $1,000 that earns 1% annually will take approximately 72 years to double to $2,000.

A global equity index fund account with a beginning balance of $1,000 that earns a 5% return on average yearly will take just over 14 years to double to $2,000.

Clearly, rate of return matters.

Clearly, with interest rates so low on cash accounts and the likelihood of long-term bond returns being low, there is increased demand for stocks given historical return patterns, as discussed.

When your money grows over time, this is called compounding. Albert Einstein called compounding the Eighth Wonder of the World for a reason. The 'Rule of 72' shows how powerful this compounding can be.

It also clearly shows that the time to start an investment plan for long-term goals is NOW since you are taking advantage of time.

Global balanced index funds – your 'go to' product for medium and long-term investing goals!

Recall that a portfolio consists of cash, bonds and equities, and their weightings will add up to 100%. The process of determining a proper asset mix is called asset allocation, and the choices made here are often a key determinant of investing success. Needless to say, these choices are important.

The longer the available timeframe we have to save for a financial goal, the more equity we can take on because we have time to ride out any market crashes and corrections – assuming that our risk tolerance is such that we can tolerate a market crash. If you can't stomach seeing your portfolio drop by 10% because you think you wouldn't be able to sleep at night or would panic (think 'sell everything'), you will need to dial back the risk level (decrease the equity weighting).

Let's look at how to approach your long-term goals first because that will make it easier to understand how to approach your medium-term goals.

For your long-term goals (think the 'big ticket' items over a decade away, like your retirement), we are going to create a portfolio of index products that contain stocks and bonds. There's not a great need for cash since it will earn next to nothing and, therefore, won't give us the growth we need – the 'Rule of 72' showed us that. We basically want to take our savings which come into an account after each payday (via autosave) and invest those dollars for long-term growth. We want those dollars invested in equities with some bond holdings to smooth out the stock market dips along the way. We want to invest in a cheap index fund which allows us to 'buy the world' for a low fee. We want a 'global balanced index fund'.

These global balanced index funds are just an outstanding solution for your long-term investing needs. They provide all of us with a 'one and done' product solution for long-term investing. They really are that effective. This is absolutely crucial to understand.

As with any fund, these global balanced index funds allow you to invest small sums on a regular basis (e.g., each pay period) to buy units of the fund. This is called dollar-cost averaging and is a proven investment strategy that allows you to acquire more units when the market is down and fewer units when the market is up. It's a great way to counteract investor fear and greed since your investing is on 'autopilot' and you are making no effort to 'time the market' (buy low and sell high). You select the asset allocation. Typically, the mix choices are as follows:

- Income – 20/80 percentage split, equities versus bonds

- Conservative – 40/60 percentage split, equities versus bonds

- Balanced – 60/40 percentage split, equities versus bonds

- Aggressive – 80/20 percentage split, equities versus bonds

If you are comfortable with greater volatility risk, taking on a higher equity weighting will likely produce greater results over the long term, taking into consideration your age, as discussed earlier. Having our 80-year-old Nana's portfolio heavily invested in an 'aggressive' global balanced index fund just can't happen.

Penny says...

We love having lots of options – the more, the better! When it comes to selecting investments, though, too many options can be overwhelming. For your long-term investing goals, embrace simplicity. A global balanced index fund can easily be your 'one and done' solution! Simple!

How do I adjust my asset mix as I get closer to my goal?

As time passes, what was once a long-term goal (such as retiring in 30 years) will become a medium-term goal; time will take care of this, as the birthdays roll by! Thus, long-term goals will become medium-term goals, and this will require you to adjust your asset allocation.

For example, a 25-year-old who wants to retire at the age of 55 might start investing $50 each payday for retirement into an 'aggressive global balanced index fund'. As the years slip by, she is able to bump this savings to $100, and then $200, per payday. Bravo! Then, once she turns 45, she can begin redirecting the new savings dollars into the 'balanced' option with 60% equity weighting to decrease her risk profile. At 50, she can then begin to shift the portfolio over to the 'conservative' or 'income' offering to further reduce risk. Why? She is only five years away from retirement and doesn't have the time to ride out another market crash. Her investment time frame is shortened now. However, she still wants to keep a portion of the portfolio invested in equities since many of those dollars will not be needed for years – so allowing the portfolio to still grow makes sense. It's worth noting that these global balanced index products automatically rebalance on a regular basis, so the designated weightings remain relatively constant over time.

This entire approach would have countless benefits such as:

• utilizing dollar-cost averaging

• avoiding market-timing errors where large amounts are invested at the wrong time (e.g., buying high)

• using global diversification (not too much Canada, eh!)

• embracing a low fee option

• establishing age-appropriate risk management

• putting autopilot investing in place

• maintaining desired asset allocation (automatic rebalancing)

• putting time on your side (get rich slow)

• avoiding a herd mentality where you crowd into a trend or sector or company at the worst possible time

• protecting you from yourself (fear and greed)

• understanding what you own

• embracing simplicity when it comes to what you own

• committing minimal time to initiate and maintain the investment portfolio

Penny says...

Each and every one of these benefits in and of itself is significant. When you are able to create an investing plan that combines all of these benefits, you are setting yourself up for long-term investing success in this crucial, crucial area of your financial life.

How do I actually go about investing in one of the global balanced index funds?

There are several primary ways to buy these 'one and done' products. The labels vary, but if you see 'index' or 'ETF' (exchange traded fund) in the fund name, along with a desciptor like 'portfolio', 'asset allocation' or 'balanced', then you are likely looking at a global balanced index product. You can purchase index funds as offered by the Big Banks. They have them, but they don't promote them because the fees are lower than their other actively managed fund offerings. There would be no brokerage account needed, and you would pay no commissions to buy or sell the units. Tangerine has some excellent options here. Be careful, by the way, that you don't select a 'Canadian balanced fund' since a fund such as this is restricted to holding only Canadian shares in its equity portion, and we want our investment dollars to roam the planet.

You can purchase a global balanced ETF from ETF providers, such as Vanguard Canada or iShares Canada. You will need a brokerage account to do this. You can accumulate your savings, and commit to purchasing these ETF products monthly or quarterly, so as to control brokerage fee commission costs. Alternatively, some brokerages offer commission-free ETF trading. The 'one and done' global balanced ETF offerings each have a management expense ratio (MER) that is typically in the .20% range, whereas the Big Bank index funds have MERs that are higher.

The following table provides details for a sampling of the Vanguard Canada[19] and iShares Canada[20] 'one and done' global balanced ETF offerings.

ETF Name	Ticker Symbol	*Target % Weightings (Equities/Bonds)
Vanguard Conservative Income ETF Portfolio	VCIP	20/80
Vanguard Conservative ETF Portfolio	VCNS	40/60
Vanguard Balanced ETF Portfolio	VBAL	60/40
Vanguard Growth ETF Portfolio	VGRO	80/20
iShares Core Income Balanced ETF Portfolio	XINC	20/80
iShares Core Conservative Balanced ETF Portfolio	XCNS	40/60
iShares Core Balanced ETF Portfolio	XBAL	60/40
iShares Core Growth ETF Portfolio	XGRO	80/20

*approximate weightings, and small cash positions may be held too

You can also use a robo-advisor.

Penny says...

Currency-hedged ETFs allow you to eliminate one type of investment risk - currency fluctuation risk - but that privilege comes at a price in the form of higher fees. Research indicates that investment returns are not materially impacted by currency fluctuations over the long term,[21] so the benefits are unclear. What is clear is that you will pay higher fees for these funds when compared to their non-hedged cousins, and higher fees hurt returns.

Robo-advisors – what's not to love!

These relatively new on-line investment management services offer global balanced index products in a 'one and done' format. They provide excellent options.

After identifying your appetite for risk and your investment tastes, the robo-advisor platforms tailor a global balanced index product for you. The fees remain razor thin (in the .5% MER range) but you can make very small investments on a regular basis, which is ideal for investors who are new to the game.

The robo-advisors' sites are also full of instructional articles designed with you in mind. They are easy to read and provide practical guidance.

You can access help, too, from their team of representatives.

Take it from two of the very best – index investing is the way to go!

Perhaps these two quotes from Warren Buffett, as captured on the cover of "The Little Book of Common Sense Investing" by index fund guru, John Bogle, might be insightful:

"A low-cost index fund is the most sensible equity investment for the great majority of investors."

"Most investors, both institutional and individual, will find that the best way to own common stocks is through an index fund that charges minimal fees."

In that same book, John Bogle encouraged readers to embrace index investing when he urged that we "Don't Look for the Needle – Buy the Haystack", where he defined the 'haystack' as the entire stock market, as available through the purchase of a low-cost index fund.[22]

Enough said.

My cousin has been loading up on pot stocks and crypto stocks. I want in on that action too!

With increased concentration comes increased risk. There are certainly a number of other investing strategies that you can use – from dividend growth strategies, to buying stocks in major indices with the highest dividend yields (such as the 'Dogs of the Dow' or 'Beat the TSX'), to stock momentum strategies, to value investing strategies, to using stock charts to spot opportunities to 'core & explore' strategies (where individual stocks or sector funds are added to an index portfolio). You can buy and sell options, you can short stocks and you can amplify risk by using margin trading where you borrow money using your existing shares as collateral in order to buy even more shares.

These strategies usually involve taking on more risk. They often require that you choose individual stocks to add to your portfolio. They also require you to manage and stay on top of your investments, and time the markets in some sense because you need to initiate buying and selling the stocks (stock rotation). You have to continually 'make bets' in an attempt to beat the index. You have to 'overweight tech' and 'underweight financials' or whatever – and be right. You have to make correct calls like this again and again, over many years, to beat the index over the long term. This involves analysis, research, luck and, most importantly, the available time to pull this off.

Chasing hot stocks = herd mentality = Fear of Missing Out = greed-driven investing = tracking stocks = lots of extra time = betting that you can beat the index = stress. The market serves up examples of this behaviour on a regular basis. Small retail investors, fueled by online community posts, pile into this or that stock in large numbers, only to watch their investment dollars disappear as those stocks fall back to normal levels.

Do you think you can beat the index – repeatedly – like for decades? Remember the vast majority of actively managed mutual funds do not beat the index over the long term. Smart, educated professionals with lots of specialized designations manage those mutual funds. With all due respect, do you really think you are going to beat the index? Even if you answer "Absolutely!", are you willing to spend the time needed to do the research to beat the index repeatedly? Yes, as discussed, Warren Buffett's Berkshire Hathaway's share performance has dusted the S&P 500 over many decades, so it is possible that you can do it, too. Are you really going to base your financial future on your ability to beat the index over the long term? If you still answer "Absolutely!", then I would encourage you to read the two quotes from Buffett in the previous lesson. Keep reading those quotes over and over until you agree with this statement: "I am going to invest in low-cost index funds as opposed to trying to beat the index."

Penny says...

Let your cousin load up on pot stocks or cryptocurrencies or gold stocks or whatever else becomes the flavour of the day. Wish your cousin good luck. You now know better. Buy the index and forget about beating it.

What do the experts predict in terms of future rates of return? These predications help us to manage our own expectations!

No one owns a crystal ball when it comes to accurately predicting future rates of return for various asset mix components.

Having said that, expert guidance can, well, guide us. Expert guidance can give us a sense of possible investment outcomes. This helps us to intelligently shape our expectations. Managing one's own expectations is absolutely crucial in many areas of life, but it's especially important when it comes to managing investment expectations.

What are experts saying, then, regarding expected long-term future rates of return for the three components – cash, bonds and equities – of the asset mix?

BlackRock is the largest issuer of ETF products on the planet. BlackRock Canada's Chief Investment Strategist, Kurt Reiman, offered these insights on projected market returns for the 2020s:

- Annualized stock market returns will be low relative to past results

    o 6.1% annualized for large-cap US equities

    o 7.3% annualized for large-cap European equities

    o 6.4% annualized for large-cap Canadian equities

    - Note that all figures are total returns which include both share appreciation and dividends but do not factor in fees nor inflation o Annualized total return for Canadian government bonds are projected to be very low at 0.4%[23]

What does this mean? Crucially, these predictions can shape our expectations with respect to the anticipated rate of return for a long-term global balanced index benchmark over the next decade. If we look at assembling a global balanced index benchmark with those four components equally weighted, that benchmark would feature a 75% equities/25% bonds split. This is a reasonable asset allocation given the decade-long timeframe. Note that the allocation for Canadian equities is a bit high given our previous discussions, but the calculation still works because the Canadian equity estimated return is between that of the US and European equities. In order to arrive at the expected annualized rate of return for that 75% equity/25% bond benchmark over the next ten years, you simply average the four estimated annual returns to get 5.05%. As noted by Mr. Reiman, this is low by historical standards. Going forward, that's a reasonable expected annualized rate of return for a global balanced index benchmark with a 75% equities/25% bonds weighting.

Penny says...

Expert predications are calling for muted long-term global balanced index benchmark rates of return going forward. This is basically because of extremely low expectations around bond rates of return. Wise investors will need to manage their expectations to account for the lower expected rates of return.

If expected rates of return are going to be lower than normal going forward, what does that mean in terms of my long-term savings goals?

We've already discussed the importance of managing expectations, so now, let's focus specifically on managing investment return expectations.

Managing expectations regarding expected investment rates of return going forward is vitally important. When you look at investment returns, two of the three variables – money invested and time – are known and can more or less be controlled. What's not known is rate of return. If investment rates of return are expected to be modest going forward, that means that you need to take action so that the other two variables do some heavier lifting in order to reach your financial goals. In other words, you should be prepared to save more money and/or do the saving over a longer period. That's the way the math works.

For a simple example of this in action, you can use a spreadsheet to calculate 'future value'. As mentioned, there are only three factors to determine future value – amount invested each period, number of periods and expected rate of return. Let's say that our goal is to reach $1,000,000 in forty years, and we want to know how much we have to invest after every two-week pay period to reach that goal if the expected rate of return is 5.05% annually (versus a more typical 7% annual rate of return).

The inputted variables would look like this:

• Rate of return/26 (since we will be making 26 biweekly deposits annually)

• Years*26 (since we will be making 26 deposits annually)

• -dollar amount (negative because the dollars are flowing away from us each time we save so as to create the total future value goal coming back to us at the end of the period…seems weird, but that's the thinking)

Any web-based financial calculator will give you the same results.

Using 5.05% as the expected rate of return, these calculations show that you will need to contribute $298 biweekly to reach $1,000,000 after forty years, whereas with a 7% 'typical' annualized rate of return, you will need to contribute only $176 biweekly over that same period to hit the goal.

This shows the shocking power of compound interest. An approximate 2% decrease in expected rate of return has caused the needed savings amount to increase by almost 70%! For an even greater shock, consider that if you saved the $298 amount and were able to earn the 7% return, the total saved would be $1.7M! That's a 70% increase in the ending investment balance. That should give you a sense of the power of compound interest.

By the way, this is also a tangible example of the effect of high actively managed mutual fund fees on long-term investing outcomes. If management expense ratio fees are approximately 2% higher on actively managed mutual funds when compared to passively managed index products, then the number crunch shows that high fees literally eat your financial nest egg over time. This should be further evidence for how important it is to drive down your investment costs. Fees matter!

Penny says...

With predicted investment rates of return being muted over the next decade, it becomes even more crucial to start saving early, save as much as you can and keep investment fees down.

If indexing works so well, how come Canadians have so much invested in Big Bank actively managed mutual funds?

Every Big Bank sells their own mutual funds. Any listing of the country's largest mutual funds (as measured by assets under management) is filled with Big Bank offerings. Virtually all these large funds are actively managed, and they generate lucrative fees for the Big Banks. How lucrative? Big Bank actively managed mutual fund fees are often two to three times higher than Big Bank passively managed (or index) product fees, as measured by a fund's management expense ratio.

Why do we have so much money invested in these Big Bank actively managed mutual funds? Big Bank staff members who are licensed to sell financial products typically do not have a professional finance designation that requires them to operate with a fiduciary duty, which mandates acting in the best interests of the client. Think about that. You may be getting financial advice from a Big Bank staff member who is under no obligation to put your interests first. It should be clear, then, why so many Canadians have been directed to put so much money into mutual funds that pay the Big Banks such hefty fees.

Ask yourself if 'profits' come before 'consumer best interests' at the Big Banks! Remember, Big Banks don't work for you.

Penny says...

Think twice before buying any Big Bank actively managed mutual fund. Big Bank competitors offer index products that come with fees that are a fraction of what's charged by Big Bank actively managed mutual funds, as measured by a fund's management expense ratio. Lower fees make a difference, and actively managed funds rarely outperform the index in the long run.

Working with a professional financial advisor helps you get better results than going it alone!

According to a recent Charles Schwab report, clients who work with advisors had much larger retirement account balances than those who chose to go it alone. Those balances – $447,000 US for those working with an advisor compared to $246,000 US for those who aren't – are telling. The clients who worked with advisors also had accounts that exhibited more diversification in their asset allocation and, furthermore, had less concentration when it came to individual equity position holdings.[24]

Why is this significant? Well, it certainly indicates that working with a professional financial advisor leads to better results.

Working with a professional advisor can certainly help protect you from yourself in terms of making rash investment decisions driven by fear or greed.

Remember that it's best to seek out an independent professional financial advisor who is under no pressure to sell a particular line of products and whose obligation is to put client interests first (fiduciary responsibility).

Given the reality of industry compensation models, don't be surprised if financial advisors aren't too interested in taking you on as a client if your portfolio is relatively small (think under six figures).

If you have a relatively small investment account, don't hesitate to move forward with a robo-advisor. Be open, too, to using a 'fee for service' independent professional financial advisor to act as your long-term financial mentor, so to speak. Working with a trusted advisor, who annually (or semiannually) reviews your robo-advisor investments, is an outstanding way to help you reach your financial goals.

Having trouble getting a non-bank financial advisor to take you on as a client? Here's why...

You're not alone in this struggle. Why is this? You know you need to save for all kinds of future financial commitments. You know you need to invest some of those monies, especially if you are serious about meeting your long-term financial goals such as retirement, paying for post-secondary schooling costs and housing. You can go to your neighbourhood Big Bank but know that their advisors often are limited to 'selling' their own expensive (i.e., high fee) Big Bank investment offerings. You have accumulated some money, but advisors don't seem to want to take you on as a client.

Sound familiar?

The issue comes down to money. Let's say you have saved diligently for a number of years and have accumulated $50,000 – awesome! Unfortunately, at a 1% rate, that pool of money will only generate about $500 worth of annual fees for your financial advisor. At that small level of annual revenue, an advisor might not be able to service your account even if the advisor wants to offer advice. At that level of revenue, head office might stipulate that the file be moved along to some type of general or call centre advisor team. You might as well walk right back to your neighbourhood Big Bank.

Robo-advisors have positioned themselves to provide financial service and advice to those with modest sums of money, and to those who are just getting started. These robo-advisors are growing rapidly; they are a fintech threat to the established Canadian financial industry given the economies of scale that come with providing automated portfolios.

Lucky enough to be working with a financial advisor now? Here's a question that you must ask...

Perhaps you have been able to secure the services of a financial advisor. You might have a personal or family connection. Regardless, we know how hard it is for professionals to beat the index over time.

If you are working with a financial advisor, are your results beating the index? We often frame this as 'beating the benchmark', which involves tracking index results based on our asset allocation and comparing our actual investment results to the benchmark results. Remember the report card example, and how you could see both a class average and your particular grade? This is along the same lines.

If your advisor is consistently able to beat the benchmark for you over many years, then your advisor is adding value. If not, then push to have your portfolio invested in index products. Your advisor will have access to these products.

This allows you to control your money, even if others are managing it for you. Empowering you in this way is one of the goals of this entire book!

By the way, if your partner is managing the family's money, ask your partner the same question. If results aren't beating the benchmark, then a discussion about shifting to index investing is the logical next step – for both of you!

Buy the dip!

We know that stock markets crash. We know there have been three significant crashes in the past two decades. We know that history tends to repeat itself.

You are almost certain to experience a stock market crash if you invest for long enough.

Market indices have always recovered from these crashes, and have moved on to higher highs. Sometimes this recovery takes years, and sometimes it happens in mere months.

Long-term investors should look at these events as buying opportunities since the indices are 'on sale', allowing you to buy pieces of world class companies when their share prices are beaten down due, in part, to investor fear. Lick your chops and have the courage to buy when others are selling – be a contrarian and you will likely be rewarded for your bravery when others are fearful.

Remember 'the trend is your friend' – stock markets go up over time since market indices are filled with large companies who have grown due to rising sales and rising profits. Great companies don't shrink themselves to greatness, so deploying extra cash to purchase index products that are filled with strong companies when they are 'on sale' is a wise move. History tells us that your future self will thank you for taking this action.

Being a buyer when it seems like everyone is selling – causing indices to plummet – takes courage. This is a time to embrace excellence when it comes to investing, as opposed to perfection. You do not want to try to 'catch the bottom' and buy at the perfect time. That is too much pressure and, in reality, virtually impossible. Instead, split any extra cash that you are able to invest into six equal parts, and commit to investing one part each month for six months to buy index products once the market bear appears. You will put dollar-cost averaging to work for you, buying more units at lower prices and fewer units at higher prices. You will also take action, which is significant because it is very, very easy to be frozen by all of the chaos that you read regarding the crash. Remember, stock market crashes are always front-page news, but markets go up over the long term. When markets are calm, create a written plan around 'buying the dip' when that opportunity presents itself – and that will definitely be 'when' as opposed to 'if'.

Investor, know thyself!

Long-term investing in the stock market using broad-based index funds has been very profitable. If past results are any indication of future results, this will continue. Stock market performance won't be predictable (nor linear) in the short term, though. Create an investment plan based on your goals featuring global balanced index funds. Use an appropriate asset mix and stick to it with an eye to your risk tolerance. Consult an independent professional financial advisor regularly to check your thinking. Remember that fear and greed impact investors in many ways, and are often an investor's worst enemy. Those emotions can drive us to panic and sell (move to cash) at precisely the wrong time or buy into market hype at precisely the wrong time, too. These can be catastrophic, wealth-destroying mistakes. Avoiding these major missteps is a key part of being a successful long-term investor. Investor, know thyself!

Key takeaways from 'Mastering Investing'

→ utilize a 'get rich SLOW' approach for long-term wealth accumulation

→ consider your personal risk tolerance when investing for long-term growth

→ realize that stock markets go up in the long term (but they can be very volatile over shorter periods)

→ keep your investment fees low since this is a key element of long-term investing success, and you have control over this piece

→ understand the importance of the three variables that drive wealth creation (amount of money invested, rate of return earned, and time) so as to put these variables to work for you

→ understand that asset mix decisions are vitally important when it comes to determining long-term investing success

→ embrace the advantages that index investing offers so that you can approach long-term investing with confidence

→ invest in global balanced index products since they open the door to achieving long-term financial goals

→ avoid investing in Big Bank actively managed mutual funds given the high fees

→ understand that robo-advisors are excellent options when it comes to investing in global balanced index products

→ automate your wealth accumulation plan – and stick to it – so as to protect yourself from fear and greed

Part IV

Mastering Your RRSP, RESP & TFSA

In 'Mastering Your RRSP, RESP & TFSA', we'll look at using these accounts through the lens of handling three significant financial challenges. The registered retirement savings plan (RRSP), the registered education savings plan (RESP) and the tax-free savings account (TFSA) all have one word in common – 'savings'. These plans can support us as we save for retirement, save for housing and save for children's education costs (if applicable). These are big costs, and we see them coming. This presents an opportunity; we can save and invest over the long term to cope with these challenges. These plans all allow for tax-sheltered growth, along with other incentives, so utilizing them offers advantages. Your future self will thank you when you have built enough wealth over time to meet these significant financial challenges.

Crucial lessons in this part of the book include understanding that RRSPs, RESPs and TFSAs have different purposes and features, understanding the tax-sheltered nature of these accounts, and seeing that workplace pension plans are rare in Canada.

The federal government has provided these accounts for us. The incentives are significant. Using them is wise, financially. The key lessons found here will allow you to utilize these accounts to maximize their benefits.

Use what they give you – tax-sheltered accounts help you cope with many huge investment worries!

As mentioned, you are going to face three significant personal financial tests in your life. These tests are 'all or nothing' – you MUST pass all of them or you are going to face financial turmoil. These tests are:

1. Saving for your retirement

2. Saving for the kids' education (if applicable)

3. Figuring out the housing affordability puzzle

Our federal government has provided us with three fantastic tools to assist us with passing these three tests.

Canadians have access to RRSPs, RESPs and TFSAs. They all have different purposes and they all have different pros and cons. Don't worry – the pros dramatically outweigh the cons!

You can't 'buy' an RRSP, RESP or TFSA. View these plans as big tax umbrellas that allow whatever you place inside the plan to grow tax free. The plans shield your assets – and the associated investment growth – from taxes while inside the plan. You open a plan, contribute to it while adhering to contribution limits, and then you have control over how the funds are invested.

Used in combination, RRSPs, RESPs and TFSAs provide Canadians with the investment vehicles to pass all three of those major financial tests! It's worth noting that TFSAs provide maximum flexibility – they can be used to save for any financial goal (not just for housing). RRSP and RESP accounts, on the other hand, have specific purposes.

Penny says...

When it comes to your personal financial toolbox, RRSPs, RESPs and TFSAs are fantastic ways to save and grow your money to pay for major, major future costs. Use what they give you!

Did we mention taxes?

We all quickly figure out that we don't get to keep all the money we make. Our friends at the Canada Revenue Agency (CRA) want their share in the form of income tax. Those taxes pay for services that benefit our society – our fantastic health care system, our superb post-secondary institutes and our excellent elementary and secondary schools are all examples of our tax dollars at work. As you well know, we pay lots of other forms of tax too. Those additional taxes – from consumption taxes (like the HST) to property taxes to 'sin taxes' (on goods such as alcohol) – add up.

The Fraser Institute analyzes this tax burden every year, and declares 'Tax Freedom Day' annually. That's the day when Canadian families theoretically have all taxes paid, and can begin to actually keep the money that they've earned that year. It usually falls somewhere in June.[1] Even during the pandemic years, with all the economic carnage and lockdowns, 'Tax Freedom Day' still managed to fall in May.[2] This gives you a sense of the tax burden that we collectively carry as Canadians, on an annual basis. We are heavily, heavily taxed.

Any discussion about investments must include a discussion about taxes. The reason is pretty clear – we want to know the after-tax value of our investment returns. Afterall, different types of investment income get taxed at different rates, and those rates vary by province, too. It's confusing.

But here's the really, really, really good news – RRSPs, RESPs and TFSAs are all tax-sheltered plans. This is so very, very important. As noted, this allows the assets in those plans to grow year by year without any tax being payable while those dollars remain in the plan. This allows the magic of compound interest to really do its job.

No workplace pension? Read this!

Canadians are having trouble saving for their retirement. Almost two-thirds of Canadians say they have little or nothing saved for retirement.[3]

You want to retire at some point. At that time, you may choose to continue to work or volunteer, but you want that to be motivated by a desire to stay connected and/or give back and/or 'stay in the game'; you don't want to continue to work well past your target retirement date because you haven't saved enough money.

There's always hoping to win the lottery, but we all know that 'hope' isn't much of a plan, and the odds are stacked against us. Hoping to receive a large inheritance is a possibility – but not a certainty. Don't build your financial future on 'hope'.

Without having contributed to a workplace pension plan, the reality is that you are likely going to have to take action in order to fund your retirement. The reality is that the person in the mirror is going to be responsible for your retirement lifestyle from a financial perspective.

How do you fund your retirement? There are government retirement monies such as Canada Pension Plan (CPP) income and Old Age Security (OAS) income but those aren't designed to give you a dream retirement, and they vary in amounts for many reasons. For example, CPP payments depend on factors such as the age you start your pension, your CPP contributions and your average earnings over your working life. At the start of this decade, the average monthly CPP amount was about $680.[4] You might get less or you might get more. You can get an estimate of your monthly CPP retirement pension payments by checking out your 'My Service Canada Account'. OAS even gets clawed back once you hit certain income levels. Both CPP income and OAS income are taxable, by the way.

There's also workplace pension income but, if you are reading this section closely, you don't have one.

Finally, there's personal savings, selling the family home or using a reverse mortgage to get access to the capital in your home.

Note that reverse mortgages allow you to essentially take out a loan using your home's equity once you are 55 years of age or older. There are no monthly loan payments to make; the loan is paid back once you decide to move or sell. The net result is that when you sell the home, you won't keep all the proceeds since you will need to pay back the loan.

If you are looking to have a comfortable retirement that includes travel and entertainment, then you have no choice but to save unless you want to sell the family home or use a reverse mortgage.

With no workplace pension, financing a retirement filled with financial freedom is going to fall on you.

RRSP – the second 'R' stands for retirement for a reason!

The registered retirement savings plan is, well, a retirement plan – and it's a good one. You 'earn' contribution room by earning income. You can find your RRSP deduction limit or contribution room by accessing your Government of Canada 'My Account' or by using the 'MyCRA' mobile app. The amount will also appear on each of your CRA 'Notice of Assessment' statements that come after each personal income tax return is reviewed.

The sweetener is that you are 'paid' to contribute to your RRSP since contributions can reduce your tax bill. If you pay into a pension plan at your workplace, your RRSP contribution room will be lower than someone who earns the same income but doesn't contribute to a workplace pension plan. This is because you are already paying into a workplace pension plan – forced retirement savings on top of the mandated CPP deductions – so the government doesn't need to offer you as much contribution space. You can also choose to establish a spousal or common-law partner RRSP where you can take steps to evenly split retirement income between the two of you.

When it comes time to withdraw the money from your RRSP, you will pay tax on those withdrawals. This is crucially important to understand. Although you can withdraw money from your RRSP, you will pay income tax on the withdrawals. Therefore, the time to withdraw money from your RRSP is during retirement, when you are theoretically in a lower tax bracket. As such, you would pay less tax. That's the best way to view the structure. Again, if you take out $60,000 during your first year of retirement, you will need to pay income tax on it; it's not tax-free cash.

In the year you turn 71 years of age, you have a choice. You can withdraw your RRSP assets, transfer them to a registered retirement income fund (RRIF) or use them to buy an annuity which will provide you with a fixed sum of money for the rest of your life.

When RRSP assets flow to you through a RRIF, amounts that are paid to you are taxable. However, while the assets remain in the RRIF, earnings in the RRIF are tax-free. The federal government requires that you withdraw money from your RRIF. The financial institution that administers your RRIF (called the 'carrier') calculates the minimum amount based on your age, as directed by the government. You can also choose to withdraw more than the minimum.[5]

You can take out up to $35,000 from your RRSP to buy or build a qualifying home through the federal government's Home Buyers' Plan. You will have to repay these funds within 15 years of withdrawing the money from your RRSP, and those payments must begin by the second year after the year you first took money from the RRSP.[6]

You can also withdraw funds from your RRSP for costs related to full-time training or education for either you, your spouse or common-law partner through the Lifelong Learning Plan. The limit here is $20,000 in total.[7] Consult the Government of Canada website for specific details.

Penny says...

Using an RRSP is a super way to save for retirement. RRSP contributions can reduce your tax bill - you are, in a sense, 'paid' to contribute - but the funds are taxable when withdrawn. Be sure to 'save the tax savings' when you do contribute or one of the major benefits is lost.

Here's how to invest your RRSP contribution dollars!

RRSPs have one purpose – to help you save for retirement. For Canadians in their 20s and 30s, that implies a long investing runway. Put simply, you are going to use a 'get rich slow' strategy (that we have already covered) by contributing what you can in a systemic way for years, and investing for growth.

You know what that looks like already.

You are going to set up a biweekly autosave program and, with those dollars, you are going to buy global balanced index products every two weeks for decades.

Don't worry about starting with small amounts. Just start.

If you are able to contribute $200 biweekly for 40 years, you will have invested a little over $200,000. If those dollars are invested in a global balanced index product which averages a 7% annual rate of return, those invested dollars will grow to over $1.1M at the end of those 40 years. If you and your partner both commit to this, that will be a retirement nest egg that is worth well over $2.2M.

But I have a workplace pension plan – so I don't need to worry about money, right?

A workplace pension plan is a rare, coveted workplace benefit in this country. They are expensive for employers to offer. This is a key factor why less than 40% of all paid workers in Canada are members of a workplace pension plan.[8] This means that the majority of our country's paid workers (over 60%) have no workplace pension plan; if you are in this group, saving for retirement is an absolute must. When it comes to enjoying workplace pension income in our retirement years, 'Hello pension, goodbye tension!' is just not the reality for the majority of Canadians.

We've looked at the two kinds of typical workplace pensions but let's review them in more detail here: one is a defined benefit pension plan (DB) and the other is a defined contribution pension plan (DC). DB plans are more common than DC plans; about two-thirds of those who have a workplace pension plan have a DB plan, versus about one in five who have a DC plan. Your employer might offer access to a 'hybrid' workplace pension plan that has both DB and DC components; approximately one in every seven paid workers in the country belong to one of these workplace pension plans.[9]

DB plans are very common in the public sector, and they are very rare in the private sector. If you work in the public sector, you likely belong to a DB plan; 80% of these workers are DB plan members. For those in the private sector, this is definitely not a reality; only 10% of those in the private sector are DB plan members.[10]

With DB plans, there's a formula that determines the retirement benefits. That's why these are called 'defined benefit' pension plans. To review an example of how DB retirement benefits are calculated, refer back to the lesson entitled 'Have a workplace benefit plan or a workplace pension plan? Understand them!' in 'Part I – Mastering the Money Mindset'.

With DC plans, your contribution rate is pre-determined – thus the label 'defined contribution' – but you will be responsible for directing how the funds are invested. The challenge here is that the pressure falls on YOU to select the appropriate asset allocation to fund your retirement. So, on the one hand, it's good to have a workplace DC pension plan, but it's also a stressor to make the investment calls. You should absolutely be seeking professional advice here.

If you belong to a workplace pension plan, you will be making mandatory contributions as part of your employment agreement, and your employer will contribute too (that's why they are expensive for employers). Be warned – these mandatory payments are large; they can often be over 10% of your gross pay. If your employer offers an optional workplace pension plan, join! Your future self will love that you made this decision.

Even if you have one of these workplace pension plans, SAVE. Let me say that more clearly; AUTOSAVE AGGRESSIVELY. Workplace pensions cover off one of the 'big three' financial tests. You still need to manage housing affordability and helping with the kids' post-secondary costs (if applicable). The number of folks with these kinds of workplace pension plans that retire AFTER their retirement date is surprising. A common reason is a lack of savings to help cover the other two big costs (school expenses and housing). A workplace pension is a wonderful income stream in retirement, but it is not a pool of money. Be aware, too, that a divorce will likely mean that your pension is going to be on the table when it comes time to finalizing a divorce settlement. Finally, don't commute your pension (i.e., take the early cash buyout option) unless there are compelling reasons such as projected limited longevity.

Penny says...

If you are a member of a workplace pension plan and you find yourself in a position where you don't earn a full year of credit, make every feasible effort to 'buy back the credit'. You can, in effect, contribute to your workplace pension plan as though you worked full-time, even though you didn't. Why would you possibly do this? After all, if you are taking an extended parental leave, for example, money will be tight. Simply put, if you don't do the buy back, you will likely have to work longer before hitting your retirement date. Your future self will be so thankful that you bought back credit when you are able to retire 'on time' with your 'full' pension amount!

RRSP withdrawals...to file away for way down the line...

RRSP dollars are best withdrawn in retirement. We've examined this.

You pay into the Canada Pension Plan (CPP) every pay period; eventually you are going to withdraw the money. Once you hit 65, you can begin these benefits with no penalty. You can also begin to receive the benefits earlier – as early as 60 – although that causes annual benefits to be reduced by over 30%. This makes sense since the CPP cash payments started flowing to you earlier.

Consider deferring the start date for your CPP benefits. You will get paid more. You actually get paid a lot more. Very, very few Canadians do this for a number of reasons, but more should. You get paid more and more for each year you defer, until you turn 70. Again, this is fair. You were able to begin collecting at the age of 65 with no penalty but you delayed the benefit, so you should then be rewarded with larger payments when they do begin.

This sets up a scenario where you can drain down your RRSP from retirement through to 70 years of age and then begin CPP payments at 70 (when the maximum CPP benefits will flow). Granted, your estimated longevity plays a part here. Your CPP varies depending on many factors, such as how long you contribute and how much you contribute, so do your due diligence here. The upside – receiving CPP benefits that are over 40% larger by deferring the start date to age 70 – is significant. You might also be able to avoid having some of your Old Age Security (OAS) benefits 'clawed back' if you can avoid large RRSP withdrawals happening at the same time as CPP income is coming in. Seek professional advice in this area since the pieces are complex. Details are available online on your My Service Canada account.

We love our kids, but they are really, really, really, really expensive! Use the RESP to help!

Having kids is expensive. We love our kids but, wow, is it ever expensive to raise one…or two…or more! The ongoing costs can be massive – sports/arts involvement, food, clothing, travel, tech, etc.

But the elephant in the room is post-secondary school costs, which can easily be $20,000 to $30,000 annually per child to attend university away from home. Worth considering is that, for some 'in-demand' fields (such as computer science, engineering and business), this can definitely be one of those costs that rises quicker than inflation. For these programs, 'user pay' pricing models may become more common. Those models just mean higher costs.

Of course, these schooling costs hit all at once. If your kids attend public schools throughout their elementary and secondary school years, there are no tuition fees nor housing costs nor living expenses nor costs to buy books. Then, all of sudden, all these costs hit. If you have more than one child attending post-secondary school at a time, these costs can skyrocket.

When do the costs hit? They hit when you are in your 40s or 50s. At that point in life, you are likely still paying down a mortgage and starting to think about retirement more and more. You may or may not have some retirement savings in place. You may or may not have a workplace pension plan. The kids' schooling costs hit you hard, right in that window. Having two kids who are both planning on moving away from home to go to university easily brings over $150,000 worth of costs – and that is in today's dollars. Project this out 15 or 20 years down the road and, with tuition costs rising even faster than inflation, you can easily be looking at well over $200,000. Gulp...

But these are costs you can see coming. These are costs that are predictable. These are costs that you can save for over time. These are costs that don't have to derail your retirement plans. This is where the RESP works so perfectly.

As an aside, and as mentioned earlier, don't ever feel that your kids 'have' to go to university. There are superb, superb programs offered through the college route. The skilled trades route is equally filled with pathways that lead to high-paying, satisfying jobs that are in demand. Remember, your child's aptitudes and passions should be the key determinant for this pathway decision.

As mentioned too, consider nearby schools as first options to cut costs if the program offerings match your child's preferences.

Penny says...

When the kids are young, childcare costs can make saving a real challenge. The federal government has made a pledge - and, more importantly, dedicated budget money - to create a national child-care program. With help from the provincial governments, this could potentially usher in $10-a-day childcare, which would be a game-changer for families struggling with substantial child care costs.[11]

Save me, RESP!

We want to help our kids with their post-secondary school costs. How are they possibly going to successfully get started in life while dragging around huge school-related debt? Ideally, we want to have them graduate debt-free so that they can launch. We want them to launch and flourish. We don't want them to boomerang back – that's not good for anyone. Yes, we want them to help cover the costs through summer jobs, paying co-operative education positions, internships, savings, scholarships and grants, but they are likely going to need additional financial support. We want to help! Half of Canadians surveyed even want to offer some help with a down payment for the kids' first home. Almost 40% of Canadians who were surveyed are actually looking at postponing their own retirement in order to offer this housing help, and a third of those polled indicated that helping the kids with their first home purchase will prevent them from being debt-free.[12]

Begin saving for your child's post-secondary school costs the month your child is born. This is the very best time to start. If those days are in the rear-view mirror, the next best time to start is right now. Full stop.

If you do this for each child, you put yourself in position to make these costs manageable. The longer you delay beginning to save, the more you will have to save each pay period. That's just the way the math works.

Penny says...

Planning on having kids? If you want the kids to launch and you want to still be able to retire on your terms, you must save for post-secondary school costs. Start this the month you hold your child for the first time. This is one of the absolute keys to retiring 'on time', whatever that means for you.

What makes the RESP so powerful?

RESPs offer sizable incentives for those who contribute to them – how does a guaranteed 20% return sound? Read on…

Begin saving for post-secondary school costs when your son or daughter is born. You will need to apply for a Social Insurance Number (SIN) from the federal government for your child. You can't apply for a SIN without a birthdate, so you really have to wait until your child arrives before applying for a SIN!

Once you have a SIN for your child, you are ready to open an RESP. You have three plan choices – family, individual or group. A family plan is a good choice, even if you presently only have one child, since you are able to add future children to the plan. Note that the children must be related to you by adoption or via a blood relationship, such as parent and child. A family plan opens the door to sharing plan earnings amongst your children. Individual plans allow only one beneficiary to be identified. Group plans are different in that your savings dollars will be pooled with other people's money and managed by a group plan dealer who invests the money on behalf of the members.[13] Consult the Government of Canada RESP website for specifics.

We'll assume that you will take control of the RESP investment decision making, which means that you have decided to go with a family plan or an individual plan.

Set up an autosave program where money comes from your operating bank account after each payday and is diverted into your child's RESP. You can start small but START your autosaving.

RESP accounts offer tax-sheltered growth in a similar way to RRSPs and TFSAs. Here's the major difference, though. The federal government pays you in cash to contribute to the plan through the Canada Education Savings Grant (CESG). You are going to get a 20% return on the first $2,500 worth of annual contributions in the form of the CESG. There is a CESG lifetime maximum of $7,200. You are going to collect that maximum amount as follows:

• Goal is to contribute $2,500 annually to each child's RESP (beginning in the year of birth) which will trigger a 20% CESG annually ($500)

• $2,500 divided by 26 biweekly pay periods is $96 per pay period

• If you do that for 14.4 years, you will have collected the maximum CESG amount of $7,200

• You will have your contributions funding the TFSA, plus the CESG monies being deposited into the TFSA, for a total of $43,200 after 14.4 years o Your contributions = $36,000 ($2,500*14.4 years)

o CESG generated = maximum amount of $7,200 ($2,500 *20% CESG*14.4 years)

o Total = $43,200 ($36,000 of your savings + $7,200 max CESG)

You have turned less than $100 per biweekly savings per child into $43,200 for each child's post-secondary school costs. That is before you invest any of the money for growth. This could easily translate to over $70,000 if invested for growth. That would put you in a position to provide significant help with covering your child's post-secondary costs – all for only $96 biweekly.

Penny says...

If you missed contributing for a year, you can still take action to get the CESG monies. The government has set the maximum CESG that can be received in any one year for a qualifying beneficiary at $1,000 (if there is unused grant room from a previous year). There are additional requirements for those beneficiaries who are 16 or 17 years of age, though, given that the CESG has been structured to encourage long-term savings.[14] Consult the Government of Canada RESP website for specifics.

You are going to invest the RESP funds – for growth!

If you skipped 'Part III – Mastering Investing', head back there before reading this part, please!

The beauty of beginning early – as soon as your child is born – to save for a child's post-secondary education is that you instantly put time to work for you. Kids just don't begin post-secondary studies on their own timetables. They progress through the school years and, after graduating from secondary school, then and only then, do they begin post-secondary studies.

The clock starts ticking the month they are born. You likely have 18 years – give or take – to accumulate the funds to finance their post-secondary school costs. Your investment timeframe is 18 years, and you will then begin to drain the money.

Recall that there are three key variables involved when it comes to amassing a large financial nest egg for a significant long-term goal, such as a child's post-secondary education costs. These variables are:

1. The MONEY that you save and invest

2. The RATE OF RETURN that you earn on those investments

3. The TIME that you have to let that money grow

We are going to tackle this using a 'get rich slow' approach which allows you to leverage the most powerful variable – time.

Saving $96 biweekly PER CHILD after every payday, year after year, is 'get rich slow', agreed?

We understand the 'Rule of 72' so we know that we need to invest our RESP money in equities so as to grow the RESP funds. Having the money just sit in a savings account for all those years is going to push that 'rate of return' down way too much. We need to grow this money.

The other lovely thing about 'get rich slow' is that you aren't as worried about stock market volatility in the early years of this 18-year journey; you have time to let any bear markets run their course before the stock markets again move to new highs.

We are going to invest the money – contributions plus the CESG – in a global balanced index product for the majority of those 18 years. You must have seen that coming, right?

My new RESP investing best friend – the robo-advisor!

You are going to save and invest every two weeks by depositing money into each child's RESP. Since you are only transferring relatively small amounts (i.e., $96) biweekly into the plan for each child, it makes little sense to pay brokerage commissions. Those are fees. We want to keep fees low. We want those small dollars to be invested so they will grow, as opposed to waiting for the money to accumulate and then depositing larger amounts. We want the $96 to move over to the RESP every two weeks – regular saving is the foundation of 'get rich slow'. We want the money invested in a global balanced index fund for all the reasons mentioned earlier. We want to turn to a robo-advisor for this.

Robo-advisors have RESP accounts. Once you have received your child's SIN, you will be able to open an RESP for that child. If you welcome more kids into this world, you can open an RESP for each of them (or add any new children to your family RESP, if you went that route). There are many Canadian robo-advisor options. Do a search to find the 'best robo-advisor in Canada' or 'largest robo-advisor in Canada'. Typically, 'largest' = 'best' with robo-advisors since their fees can be driven even lower because they have more 'assets under management' than competitors, so the costs per user can go down. Go to their website and you will see their RESP account option. Move through the steps to open one for your child. Set up an autosaving program so that the day after payday, $96 will be transferred from your operating bank account into the RESP account(s).

You will be able to select the asset mix for the RESP dollars. The choices will reflect increased exposure to equities. The choices will look something like 'conservative', 'balanced' and 'growth' along a risk continuum. We discussed this in detail in 'Part III – Mastering Investing', but let's revisit some asset allocation options, as they pertain to robo-advisors.

'Conservative' would typically mean a lighter emphasis on stocks such as a portfolio that contains a 30% stock/70% bond asset allocation. Here's what 'conservative' might look like:

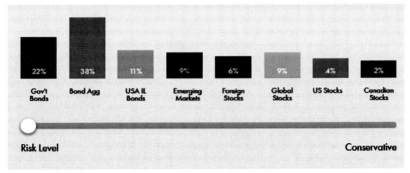

'Balanced' would typically mean a middle-of-the-road emphasis on stocks such as a portfolio that contains a 60% stock/40% bond asset allocation. Here's an example of 'balanced':

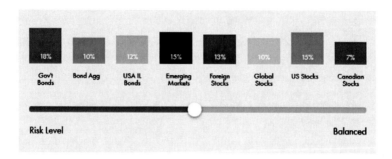

'Growth' would typically mean a heavier emphasis on stocks such as a portfolio that features an 85% stock/15% bond asset allocation. Here's a look at a 'growth' example:

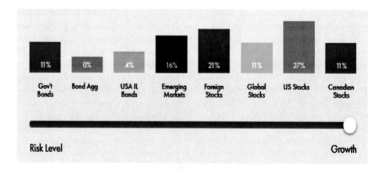

In some cases, totals add up to 101% due to rounding.[15]

For the early years of your kids' RESPs, go for 'growth'! Then, dial back the risk!

'When' you open an RESP matters. Opening one right after your child is born gives you an investment window of 18 years, or so. Given this, during the early years, your $96 deposits should be invested for maximum growth. Even if you are fairly risk averse, you should avoid a conservative asset mix since time is such a valuable ally.

Consider investing the funds in a 'growth' portfolio for the first decade.

Then, for approximately the next four and a half years (which is the additional amount of time it will take to harvest the maximum CESG), direct new deposits into a 'balanced' option.

At the 14.4-year mark, you can then dial down the risk. At this point, you can stop the deposits since the CESG has been maximized. Contact the robo-advisor and instruct them to begin liquidating the portfolio – perhaps 5% a month – such that you have the entire portfolio out of the stock and bond markets once your child is 16 or 17.

You want to have the portfolio in cash at that point. A stock market crash the year before your child graduates is not going to leave enough time for the portfolio to recover before you need the money!

Do this for each of your children. Here's what it would look like:

Child's Age	Stock/Bond Ratio	Typical Fund Choices/Names
Birth to 14.4 years of age	**Choice 1:** 80%/20%	Growth
	Choice 2: 60%/40%	Balanced
	Choice 3: 40%/60%	Conservative
Beyond 14.4 years of age	Start to move to cash (e.g., sell 5% of the funds monthly)	High-interest savings account or GICs

One of the kids is about to begin post-secondary school. Show me the money!

Here's a little secret – saving for your kids' post-secondary costs is going to put you in a position to retire early! How? Well, if you have patiently saved for years for schooling costs and invested for growth as per our earlier discussions, then you are a saver. You will be saving for retirement then, too. You will also have gotten a handle on the housing puzzle. You will be in that late-40s to mid-50s age range, give or take, and you will now be able to contemplate retiring because you will have the financial piece figured out – BRAVO!

Now that one of the kids is beginning the post-secondary education years, let's look at how you are going to go about withdrawing the RESP funds. Based on our earlier conversation, you have dialed back the risk significantly so even a stock market meltdown won't hurt you now. The RESP portfolio is basically sitting in cash, more or less.

When any of the kids begin post-secondary programs, you will need to submit an 'RESP withdrawal form' to the RESP promoter (the financial institution that you used to set up the RESP). You will also need to provide the RESP promoter with a statement from your son's or daughter's educational institute which will include information such as the post-secondary institute name, the enrolled program, full-time or part-time status and length of program, to mention a few. Post-secondary institutes can usually generate these statements automatically now. Students can often just access their student portal, and print the statement for themselves. Regardless, you need that statement from the school, and it must be submitted with your completed RESP withdrawal form.

Contact the RESP promoter in advance of post-secondary enrollment to learn about documentation requirements associated with plan withdrawal requests. A good rule of thumb is to check that the expenses are reasonable to further the student's studies. This obviously provides a great deal of flexibility, and receipts aren't typically required. Again, check with the RESP promoter in advance of enrollment to avoid any surprises here.

You will need to identify the source of the funds for each and every withdrawal. Each RESP withdrawal has two possible components – the invested funds (contributions) and an Educational Assistance Payment (EAP), which is made up of the Canada Education Savings Grant (CESG) money and investment growth. Contributions are your own money and, since you do not get a tax break for making contributions to an RESP, you do not pay income tax on these contributions when they are withdrawn. Again, you need to identify the source of the RESP withdrawal each and every time that you initiate a withdrawal. Note that any given withdrawal can be funded by either (or both) of the components – contributions and EAP – so you have total control over this piece.

EAP monies will be taxable in the student's hands. But students will likely have little income during these years, and there are high educational cost deductions from a tax perspective. The kids, therefore, are not likely going to face a big tax bill when these funds flow to them.

The net result is that the RESP can grow tax free until the funds are withdrawn, but the growth is taxable in the student's hands. Strategically spreading out these withdrawals over the post-secondary years sets up the preferred scenario where a small (or even no) income tax liability is created.

There are some limits to consider when making RESP withdrawals. For example, during the student's first 13 consecutive weeks of enrollment, EAP dollars are capped at $5,000 for full-time students and $2,500 for those studying part-time.[16] Consult the Government of Canada RESP website in advance so as to ensure that you are aware of these limitations.

As mentioned, this is ground zero for 'your future self will thank you' since you will be approaching retirement age when the kids are coming up on their post-secondary education years – but you will not have to worry about their school costs.

Talk to your kids about their RESP accounts so that they can watch the progress over the years. It's wise to let them know that you are saving and investing for this large cost, but they will need to bring some money to the table, too. By all means, sit down with them when they are old enough to go over the entire process – why you are saving, how you are investing, the returns, etc. This also opens the door to all sorts of discussions around affordability. For example, if the kids are looking to move into a house as opposed to living in residence, encourage them to look online for quality used furnishings! Another great money-saving strategy is selecting a post-secondary institute that's geographically close by, if available, so as to attend an appropriate program while living at home.

Penny says...

It's important to check out the Government of Canada's RESP website and learn the basics of RESPs. There are nuances that are important to understand, such as how to go about setting up an RESP and the availability of the Canada Learning Bond for lower-income families, for example.

TFSA – The 'tax-free' in the name 'tax-free savings account' is really important!

The TFSA is far, far more flexible than both the RESP and RRSP. Why? RESP accounts are designed for one purpose – to save for your kids' post-secondary schooling costs. RRSP accounts are designed for one purpose – to save for your retirement. When it comes to TFSAs, you can use them for ANY type of financial goal and there are no age specifications nor rules regarding when the monies need to be removed from the account. For example, if you want to save for your next home, the TFSA works perfectly for that. You can certainly use your TFSA for short-term and medium-term saving goals, too. For those dollars, be cognizant of appropriate investments given the timeframes involved, as discussed in 'Part III – Mastering Investing'.

Why are TFSAs so ideal for long-term investing? The first two letters provide the answer – TF stands for 'tax-free'. You can invest knowing that the gains that you see in your TFSA will be yours. The TFSA will shelter those monies from income tax. What you see is what you get! If you can grow your TFSA to $200,000 and want to withdraw the money, every penny of that will go to you with no income tax payable – NONE. Why is this? You don't get the benefit of a tax reduction when contributing to a TFSA as you would with an RRSP, so you don't pay income tax on the withdrawals. The benefit is tax-free growth with maximum flexibility around how you choose to use the withdrawn dollars.

This should be your 'go to' tax-sheltered account choice for all your long-term saving goals, except for saving for your kids' schooling costs and saving for your retirement. Having said that, you can certainly use your TFSA to save for those two goals, but the benefits of RESP and RRSP accounts make them the ideal choices for those two saving purposes.

If you want to save for your retirement using your RRSP account and you are in the early stages of your career, you might want to hold off on making RRSP contributions. The reason is that you get a tax break when you contribute, but you have to pay tax when you withdraw the funds in retirement. Theoretically, you will be earning less in retirement and will, therefore, pay less in tax on the RRSP withdrawals since you will be in a lower tax bracket. To really get the most 'bang for the RRSP contribution buck', you want to make your contributions when you are making a higher income. Don't get me wrong – contributing to an RRSP is a great idea but you may want to wait until your income is higher. You can always save inside your TFSA during the early stages of your career and then transfer money from your TFSA into your RRSP during your higher earnings years. That's a good strategy. If you are maxing out your TFSA contributions, then contributing to your RRSP makes great sense.

Penny says...

The federal government has given Canadians three powerful tax-sheltered tools to assist us with long-terms savings. The three – RRSPs, RESPs and TFSAs – all have different features and different purposes. Using each of these tools in a co-ordinated way is one of the best ways to ensure personal financial success!

Time...so powerful! Use it or lose it!

When it comes to long-term investment goals, we know that there are really three key components:

1. Dollars invested (that's the saving piece)

2. Rate of return (recall the 'Rule of 72' discussion)

3. Time (the longer, the better)

The lesson here is start saving as early as possible for long-term savings goals. You will never regret this. When you start saving early, and combine that with long-term investing for growth inside tax-sheltered accounts (such as RRSPs, RESPs and TFSAs), you are well, well on your way financially.

For example, let's say that you and your partner commit to saving $100 each per biweekly pay period, and that money grows at 7% annually in a tax-sheltered account. After 40 years, that will grow to over $1M. What happens if you start late and commit to that saving and investing program for only 20 years? You might assume that the total final amount will be cut in half, which would seem reasonable. However, the final amount would only grow to slightly over $225,000.

How is that possible? That's the power of compound interest.

Penny says...

Albert Einstein famously said that "Compound interest is the eighth wonder of the world. He who understands it, earns it; he who doesn't, pays it." Who's going to argue with Albert Einstein?

You and your TFSA contribution room...

While you 'earn' RRSP contribution space, you 'age into' TFSA contribution space. Are you a Canadian who is now 18 years of age or older? Congratulations – you have TFSA contribution space! If your 18th birthday is now in the rear-view mirror and you've never opened a TFSA, let alone contributed to one, don't worry! You have been accumulating TFSA room each year since you turned 18, and that contribution room rolls over and increases year after year. Isn't Canada great!

Back in 2009 when the TFSA debuted in Canada, you were allowed to contribute up to $5,000 annually. The limit was bumped up to $5,500 as of 2013. The year 2015 saw the limit go to $10,000 for one year only before returning to $5,500 in 2016. The limit was moved to $6,000 in 2019. Future annual limit increases will be done in $500 increments based on inflation, which will allow the TFSA to stay relevant for Canadians as a powerful savings tool.

If you have never contributed to a TFSA, you have $75,500 worth of contribution room as of 2021 as long as you were 18 years of age or older back in 2009. If your partner is of a similar vintage, then you have a combined $156,000 worth of contribution space as of 2021.

We know that you will NOT receive a tax credit for contributing to your (or anyone else's) TFSA, as would be the case with RRSP accounts. This actually is a huge bonus since the CRA views the contributions as coming from money that was taxed already (funded with money from your job, for example). As a result, the CRA won't tax you on any withdrawals. It bears repeating that this sets up a powerful pair of advantages – tax-sheltered growth with no tax payable on withdrawals. Remember, 'what you see is what you get' when it comes to your TFSA balance. When compared to an RRSP, this is a very significant difference since RRSP withdrawals are taxed.

Like an RRSP, there are penalties associated with over-contributing to your TFSA. That's fair. There is an allowable over-contribution amount of $2,000 for your RRSP, but you can't deduct those excess contributions from taxable income. Having said that, those dollars can be invested for tax-free growth, so planning to 'permanently' carry an over-contribution of $2,000 in your RRSP is a wise move. No such opportunity exists for your TFSA.

TFSA withdrawals...

You can take money out of your TFSA with no tax consequences. Withdrawals will be added to your TFSA contribution room the following year, and you can replace the amount that you withdrew in the same year if (and only if) you have TFSA contribution space available. You can always check your TFSA contribution room status online on the myCRA portal.

Dipping into your TFSA unexpectedly...don't do it!

Over time, you're going to have success with the 'get rich slow' process inside your TFSA. It works since you have put in place key elements of long-term wealth accumulation – autosaving for years inside a tax-sheltered account and then investing for growth using low-cost index products. If you and your partner take this on, it will really work. At some point, you are going to eye the considerable balance in your TFSA and muse to yourself about 'borrowing' some money from the account for some unplanned purpose.

Here's an alternative.

Identify those eventualities during your regularly-scheduled financial reviews and start saving for them. If it's important to you, save for it.

If one of your saving goals inside your TFSA is a down payment for a larger home and that time arrives, by all means, withdraw the money from your TFSA! What good is saving if you don't use your targeted savings when the targeted need arises? However, resist the temptation to dip into your TFSA for something unexpected. Once you do it once, you will be more prone to do it again and again. If you and your partner are out of TFSA contribution room, then save in an 'open' or 'unregistered' account. Any income (interest, dividends or capital gains) will be taxable but you can still save this way.

A little case study might be instructive…

There are a lot of pieces here – RRSP, RESP, TFSA, RRIF – HELP!

If you have kids, save using an RESP to grab the 20% guaranteed CESG money. That is a no-brainer!

The RRSP (and then the RRIF) is 'single-purpose'. You use an RRSP to save for retirement. It's a great tool, but the money inside the RRSP will be taxed on the way out.

The TFSA, however, provides maximum flexibility and generous contribution limits.

Here's a case study demonstrating how the TFSA and RESP can be used in concert over a key decade and a half. Here are the facts:

• A family has two adults and two young kids

• Both adults commit to autosaving

    o Each open TFSAs for retirement savings

    o RESP accounts are opened for both the kids to fund post-secondary costs

    o Autosaving will be set up to automatically occur after each biweekly pay period (26 times annually)

• Contributions are made to each adult's TFSA up to the annual current limit of $6,000 (ignore past unused contribution room)

    o $6,000 *2 adults =$12,000 / 26 pay periods = $461.54 per pay period (A)

• Contributions of $2,500 are made to each child's RESP for 14.4 years to trigger the annual 20% CESG of $500 ($2,500 contribution * 20% = $500) to the allowed maximum of $7,200 of total grant received per child ($500 * 14.4 years = $7,200)

    o ($2,500 + $500) * 2 kids = $6,000 / 26 pay periods = $230.77 per pay period (B) o Note that the adults need only contribute $2,500 * 2 kids / 26 pay periods = $192.31 per pay period since the other $500 * 2 kids / 26 pay periods = $38.46 comes from the CESG monies

• Total invested biweekly for 14.4 years = A+B = $461.54 + $230.77 = $692.31

   o Total monies from adults invested biweekly = $692.31 - $38.46 = $653.85

• Given the long-term nature of the investment goals, the funds are invested in a global balanced index product with very low fees which average a 5% annual rate of return

• Total value at the end of 14.4 years = $379,086.02

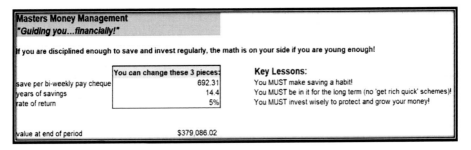

That money can be used to significantly assist the kids with post-secondary school costs, and the residual money will leave a wonderful base for the beginnings of a quality retirement fund. Don't forget that the case study only has the couple saving for approximately 15 years; results will be drastically improved with a longer period of savings. Still, accumulating a portfolio worth over $375,000 in under 15 years is impressive!

Key takeaways from 'Mastering Your RRSP, RESP and TFSA'

→ utilize RRSPs, RESPs and TFSAs so as to enjoy the benefits of tax-sheltered investment growth

→ understand that these accounts have different purposes

→ realize that workplace pension plans aren't common in Canada which means that many Canadians must take responsibility for their own retirement savings

→ embrace equities when investing RRSP, RESP and TFSA dollars for long-term growth

→ understand that RESP accounts provide guaranteed 20% returns

→ realize that your TFSA withdrawals will be yours to keep (while tax will be payable on RRSP withdrawals)

→ use RRSPs, RESPs and TFSAs in unison for many years to simultaneously work towards achieving key, long-term financial goals

Part V

Mastering Your Ride

In 'Mastering Your Ride', we'll be looking at taking control of vehicle ownership decisions. For many, vehicles are status symbols. It's so common to equate financial success with what we drive. Seeing a friend post a picture of their new truck makes us instantly think that they must be doing well financially. We seldom see anyone post the payment plans, though. It's worth noting that massive vehicle payments can hamper our ability to save adequately, and can even hurt our chances to qualify for a mortgage down the road.

Crucial lessons in this part of the book include understanding that vehicles depreciate (so they really aren't investments), understanding that dealerships want us to lease new vehicles, and how to go about buying a quality used vehicle.

Make no mistake, a vehicle purchase is a major financial decision. In fact, it's often one of the first ones we make so, in many ways, it can set a precedent for us around how we approach major purchases, and the corresponding debt. The key lessons found here will allow you to take control of the vehicle purchasing process for the rest of your life.

My neighbours and friends all have new, fancy vehicles – I want one too!

FOMO – fear of missing out – lives right here.

Have you ever noticed the number of luxury, high-end cars and trucks on our roads and highways? Perhaps you have even spotted them right in your own neighbourhood. You can sometimes spot two of these vehicles (not just one) parked on a driveway in what we would consider the 'middle class' parts of town. Vehicles are status symbols for us. Driving a fantastic car or truck messages something about us to others; it announces that 'I've made it'. That's what the auto manufacturers' advertisements all show, so it must be true, right?

For many, many Canadians, this is ground zero for their first major financial mistake – and their second and third and – well, you get it.

Here's a little secret – your neighbours didn't 'buy' those vehicles. Some of those high-end toys cost over $80,000 each and, for those households with two of these vehicles, that means a price tag of over $160,000. People don't walk into dealerships and hand over $160,000. Instead, they lease those vehicles (leasing is just code for 'renting', really) or finance them through car loans. There are often enticing dealer promotions that require minimal down payments and feature payment schedules that are amortized (finance talk for 'spread out') over sometimes seven or more years. These long amortization periods result in lower payments, and lower payments are very, very appealing to consumers!

When it comes to those high-end vehicles you see on the roads, it's important to realize that many haven't been bought with cash; frequently, they've been leased or financed with small, small down payments.

Vehicle ownership is expensive – ridiculously expensive!

If the only cost associated with car or truck ownership was the purchase price, that would be one thing. Those costs are, unfortunately, only the start of the story. As a matter of fact, vehicle ownership is ridiculously expensive. In addition to the purchase price and financing costs (interest built into the car loan or lease), you've also got to deal with the maintenance costs, insurance payments and fuel costs. Nowadays, a new set of tires can easily run over $1,000 installed, and winter tires involve storage costs and seasonal tire change charges, too. Then there's the parking costs, which sometimes take the form of having to buy a parking space in a condo complex. Those who need to park downtown in our big cities quickly discover that they pay a small fortune each day to parking lot attendants for the privilege of parking a car or truck near their workplace.

However, the 'cost' of owning a car or truck goes beyond those of the owner. Think of the environmental impact associated with manufacturing and operating a machine that emits harmful gases into our environment.

Having said that, the owner of an electric vehicle (EV) still has many of the same costs as the owner of a combustion engine vehicle; after all, EVs are still vehicles.

Do you even need a vehicle? Families that decide to move from two vehicles down to one notice the significant savings immediately. With the prevalence of ride-sharing options, expanding public transit and the work-from-home movement, do you really need to own a vehicle anymore? Could it be that your family no longer really needs to own two vehicles? Do you see walking, biking, roller-blading, or even skating (where available in the

Great White North) to work or school as a possibility for you or other family members?

The dollars that can be freed up can be redirected to RRSPs, TFSAs and RESPs, and invested for long-term growth. Perhaps that's the way you can retire early. It's something worth considering on many, many levels – not the least of which is environmental stewardship.

Penny says...

EV sales are rapidly rising. Deloitte is forecasting that the annual compound growth rate for EV sales will be nearly 30% over the next ten years, with EVs securing approximately one-third of the total new car sales market by 2030.[1]

You don't need a new vehicle!

Let's assume that you have decided that you do, indeed, need a vehicle. Since vehicles are so expensive, manufacturers and their dealerships having been finding ways to lower monthly payments for consumers. That should make sense. Marketers are very, very good at taking large purchases and chunking the cost into bite-sized monthly costs. As a matter of fact, manufacturers have even shifted to displaying weekly lease payments (as opposed to monthly or biweekly payments) so as to create the illusion of better affordability.

For the consumer, it's all about cash flow. A consumer might want a high-end car, but can't come up with the needed money to even carry monthly car loan payments. The sales representative can offer leasing as an option, and all of a sudden you will hear something like this: "We can get you into this car for only $150 a week. You can afford that, right?" You are instantly put on the defensive and want to show that, of course, you can afford that weekly payment, so you sign on the dotted line. Note that $150 a week equates to paying almost $8,000 annually to essentially 'rent' the car since you won't own it when the lease ends.

That's why you see so many new, luxury vehicles all over the roads and in your neighbourhood. Those payments add up, by the way; if you purchase two vehicles this way, then two of those payments can easily end up being well over $1,000 a month. Those are perpetual payments as you'll see in a moment.

Let's look at how this works from the dealership's perspective. You just leased a new car. That means that you are going to need to have it serviced on a regular basis (they will encourage you to have that service done at the dealership since "we know our cars so well") in order to honour the lease agreement. You will have to be careful not to put too many kilometres on the vehicle since you will face paying a heavy surcharge for extra usage, based on a kilometre threshold found in the lease. Your lease will expire in something like four, five or six years. When that happens, you will come right back to the dealership and drop off the car. This means that you now need another car, and are sitting right in the dealership. This is an ideal scenario for the dealership; literally, it's perfect. It creates a continuous flow of return customers (every retailer's dream come true) for the dealership because when one lease ends, it's immediately replaced with another.

We need to take drastic action to change the way the game is played here. As a matter of fact, we're going to do the absolute opposite of what's just been described.

Instead of leasing a new vehicle, we want to buy a vehicle that has just come off a lease. We want to buy a quality used vehicle.

Penny says...

One of the earliest major financial mistakes you can make in life is acting on the belief that, somehow, you 'deserve' a new vehicle once you graduate from college or university. It's easy to see where this idea originates: auto manufacturers offer discounts targeting recent graduates, and lenders advertise auto loans targeting this group, too. Avoid this trap! Buying a quality used vehicle is a wise move if you decide that you do, indeed, need a vehicle!

You don't 'invest' in a vehicle – they don't go up in value

You may hear a vehicle advertisement or sales representative mention that a particular vehicle is a 'great investment'. It's not a great investment. That car or truck is going to go down in value unless it's a vintage, antique model, which you're probably not considering at this point in your life. That vehicle is going to go down in value for many reasons that are easy to identify, such as 'wear and tear' and age.

Cars and trucks depreciate. They go down in value. Good investments appreciate, or go up in value. These vehicles, therefore, are not investments. That depreciation can create a tax write-off, if you own your own business and use the vehicle for business purposes. Even after saying that, let's be clear that cars and trucks aren't investments.

Aren't used vehicles just money pits?

We know that 'leasing new vehicles' is a dealership's business model of choice, so we understand that breaking that cycle involves doing the opposite – which involves buying quality used vehicles. In our society, anything and everything that is 'used' comes with a stigma. With used vehicles, though, we have a built-in advantage – use the 'leasing new vehicles' business model to your advantage.

Be intentional about buying one of those quality vehicles that is coming off a lease, and is now sitting on the dealer's 'used car' lot.

The previous 'owner' (the leaseholder) of a leased vehicle has been driving that leased car or truck 'gently' for the length of the lease. Why? They know that they don't own the vehicle! They know that they must keep the kilometres under a certain limit, or face paying a stiff charge when the lease expires. They know that they need to have regularly-scheduled maintenance performed on the vehicle, or risk a hefty penalty when they hand over the keys. That penalty is assessed when mechanical problems are spotted that can be traced back to irregular maintenance.

The vehicles that are coming off leases have been treated well, and often have low kilometres on them.

NEVER buy a used vehicle from a car rental agency!

Now is a good time to mention that you are also able to buy used vehicles from car rental agencies. Avoid these cars and trucks, no matter how good the price looks. Why? Have you ever been in a rental car with your dad on some family trip? Something happens to dads when they get behind the wheel of a rental. It's as if they've become some type of race car driver. Those poor vehicles get driven that way, time and time again. Some parts wear out more rapidly when vehicles are driven aggressively. The car rental agency knows that they are going to 'roll the fleet' at some point in time, based on the age of any given vehicle or the number of kilometres driven. As such, they aren't 'long-term' owners, and don't plan on spending dollars doing major maintenance work on vehicles. They plan on selling them. Take a pass on these vehicles.

Help me find a quality used vehicle!

You will need to do some work on your side first. How much can you bring to the table as a down payment? What's your monthly payment threshold? How are you going to finance the purchase? If you use a line of credit, how much will you pay on the debt each pay period to decrease the debt?

Your vision here should be to find a four-year-old vehicle that is coming off of a lease and to own it for an additional six years. That's right, you are going to trade it in once it is ten years old! However, you will want to have it totally paid off after only three years, after which you will own it with no debt.

Let's say you are looking at a quality used vehicle that will cost you $15,000 in total. You have $3,500 for a down payment so you will need to finance the difference, which is $11,500. Your goal is to have the vehicle paid off in three years which equates to thirty-six monthly payments. Your payments will end up being approximately $350 monthly, using a 6% annual interest rate. Remember, you don't have to finance the vehicle purchase through the dealership. Using your line of credit provides a cheap source of financing, for example. You will need to be disciplined to eliminate the balance owing on the line of credit in three years as outlined. Setting up automatic monthly payments is an excellent strategy to help you achieve that goal.

How much money can you save with this strategy? An example might be helpful. In 2008, I bought a four-year-old van for $18,000 (pre-tax) that was manufactured by a highly-regarded Japanese auto manufacturer. I found the original sales invoice in the glove compartment. That van originally sold for $45,000. It had depreciated to the tune of $27,000 (or 60% of its original value) over four years. Someone else paid for that depreciation. Don't buy new vehicles and you will never pay for all that 'new car' depreciation either!

Let's go in with our eyes wide open here. You are, indeed, buying a used vehicle, and it may not have any 'new vehicle' transferable warranty remaining on it when you buy it. You are looking, therefore, for a quality vehicle from an excellent manufacturer, since you are going to own that vehicle for six years (from years five to 10 of the vehicle's life).

Be certain, therefore, to consult publications from an independent source (such as 'Consumer Reports') that ranks used vehicles annually. These sources will often list 'best used cars' by budget threshold and vehicle type, given past repair and reliability scores. The key piece here is 'independent' – these organizations aren't paid by the manufacturers, so bias is removed. You can often access these publications from the comfort of your own home by using your public library's website. Simply enter your library card information to gain access to the library's databases. It just doesn't get much easier than that!

Once you have a shortlist of vehicle make, model and model years that you want to consider, and you have a budget in mind, then – and only then – should you actually start looking for vehicles. Don't be afraid of looking at vehicles that have been driven 60,000 or 80,000 or even 100,000 kilometres. Remember that those vehicles have been well-maintained, and quality auto manufacturers build engines to last for well over 250,000 kilometres. You are invariably going to see cheaper used vehicles, but put your faith in the independent research. Remember that you are looking for a quality used vehicle, and they will be listed for higher asking prices for a reason – they are in demand. You will pay more to buy a better-quality vehicle in order to limit the chance of having nasty ongoing repair costs. Paying a little more for a quality vehicle will pay for itself, again and again.

Web-based car search sites are common. Sites (such as Autotrader.ca) allow you to search based on virtually all parameters, including distance to your home, so as to make the search more practical.[2]

Be patient! Remember that four or five years ago, good folks were leasing new vehicles every single day. Those leases are expiring, and those dealerships want to make some more money by selling those vehicles. More inventory hits the dealership 'used car lots' each week.

Penny says...

Avoid buying a vehicle that has accident history. This introduces way too many unknowns. Yes, the price will be lower but you many, indeed, be buying a 'money pit' once you go down this road. There's no reason to do this. Remember that more inventory will hit those used car lots every week.

I found a great used vehicle in my budget range. Now what?

You likely found a vehicle at a dealership as opposed to a 'private seller'. Why? Dealers like to make money from lots of different revenue sources. Yes, they sell vehicles, but they also have financing departments that offer financing options to customers, along with service departments that do repairs and maintenance. They also have used car lots where they make money selling traded-in vehicles and lease returns. They hold on to quality trade-in vehicles and lease returns since they can sell them under their dealership banner. The vehicles that aren't up to their standards (or are, perhaps, not the same make that the dealer sells as 'new') are sent to 'auction' where they are picked up by other dealerships.

Call about the vehicle before going to see it. What's the history? Remember, you will take a pass if it's been in any accidents. Ask to have the 'car history report' emailed to you. You want to ask about previous owners and vehicle history; it's wonderful to learn that a particular vehicle of interest has had one owner who leased the vehicle and had it serviced at the dealership. The car history report will tell you all of this and will also show service dates, accident history and more. Are there any extra costs such as 'administration fees' upon the sale? Does it come with snow tires? Is there any manufacturer's warranty left on the vehicle? Knowing the answers to these questions in advance of seeing the vehicle is important.

If you like what you hear, book a test drive. Don't feel pressured into making an offer. Call your insurance company to get a quote on the cost of insurance coverage for the vehicle. You will need the vehicle information number (VIN), which is found in the car history report and on the dashboard (visible through the front windshield).

If you like the feel and look of the vehicle after the test drive, ask if you can take it to YOUR mechanic to have your mechanic look it over. The dealership will say 'yes' to this.

Contact your mechanic. Don't have a mechanic? Call a local, independently-owned shop and ask if they can do an inspection for you in advance of making an offer to purchase. They will say 'yes'. You want to get to know your mechanic and patronize that shop for years. You want a relationship with that shop. You want your mechanic to know your car or truck. You want to explain that, if you buy this vehicle, you plan on bringing it back for service for years. You want to be a good customer and get to know the staff and owner. You want to be a 'relationship builder' in this area!

Penny says...

Many auto service shops also sell vehicles. If you are looking to purchase a quality used vehicle and are not under time pressure, consider speaking with your mechanic to see what's available at the car dealer auction. The auction provides access to many vehicles on a regular basis. Lease returns are available in large quantities. There's value here; fees would be involved, but the final price might be lower than what you would pay to buy a vehicle on your own. Also, the car dealer auction provides condition reports for each vehicle to assist with transparency so as to lower buyer risk.

I'm ready to make an offer!

Have you ever heard of the phrase 'knowledge is power'? It will be on full display here. Your mechanic will report the results of the vehicle inspection to you; this will be invaluable. This knowledge will level the playing field since you will now know what the dealership knows based on your mechanic's report. For example, your mechanic can tell you how much life is left on the tires and brakes. Note that vehicles can pass the 'safety test' but that doesn't guarantee that the brakes and tires are not in need of being replaced at some point in the not-to-distant future. The mechanic can tell how well the vehicle has been maintained – their expert eyes can spot telltale signs of good (or bad) maintenance history. Ask the mechanic if this is a vehicle worth purchasing, and if the dealership's asking price is fair. Remember, your mechanic is an expert in this field!

As mentioned, what you learn from the mechanic's inspection will be tremendously useful to you. If the mechanic tells you to take a pass on the vehicle based on what's uncovered in the inspection, don't view this as a setback. Instead, think of the barrels of money that you just saved yourself by having the inspection done before you bought the vehicle. If you do decide to go forward with an offer to purchase the vehicle, you know that you are on a level playing field with the dealership. You have done your homework and the dealer knows that you have done your homework. You are ready to make an offer. Make an appointment with the dealership's sales representative with whom you have been in contact and go in with a plan. Bring someone along with you for support, since 'two heads are often better than one'.

Let's say that the ask price is $16,000. You know from your mechanic that the vehicle will comfortably pass the safety test, but the tires need to be replaced next season and the brakes will need service in the next six months. You won't be offering to pay $16,000 then. You will explain what you know and offer an amount below the ask price. Based on your mechanic's suggestion, you might come in with an initial offer of $14,000, knowing full-well that you are willing to pay $15,000 for the car. Don't forget that you will pay HST on top of the agreed-upon price, so take that into account, too.

Don't be surprised if the sales representative will need to leave the office to take your offer to the sales manager. This is a typical strategy designed to unease you. Hold tight. One strategy is to get up and leave the office if the sales representative leaves. Walk around the showroom. Go outside for a breath of fresh air. Don't let yourself sit there and get nervous. Having someone with you comes in handy for support; the dollar amounts are big, and it's easy to get nervous since you are likely not used to this kind of a negotiation.

Remember that they want to sell the car. They will come back with a counter offer. It might be within a few hundred dollars of what you are willing to pay. At that point, you can counter offer again or even take their offer.

You can also walk away if the dealership team members are not willing to drop the price to your liking. They have your contact information, so don't be surprised if you get a callback the next day, especially if they have had the car on the lot for some time.

Remember, you don't have to buy that particular vehicle. It's a business transaction. As mentioned, having someone with you for moral support is helpful. This can be a stressful experience, but the savings compared to getting a new vehicle are beyond substantial.

I bought a great vehicle today!

Buying a quality used vehicle is a wise move! Once you have made the purchase, you will need to make a down payment. The full price will be payable at the time of pick-up. Call your insurance company and they will issue you a temporary insurance certificate that you will need to bring when it comes time to pick up your vehicle. You will be issued license plates also.

Don't forget to drop around to your mechanic with a suitable gift to say 'thanks' for the assistance. Yes, you will have paid for 30 to 60 minutes or so of labour, but that gave you the confidence and the peace of mind that you needed to get through the negotiation!

Consult with your mechanic about a service schedule for your vehicle. Follow that schedule. Regular maintenance beats the alternative, which involves expensive repairs! Budget for repair costs – both small and large. Remember, you are going to keep the vehicle for six years so plan accordingly.

How does a 'trade-in' change the game?

If you have a vehicle now, consider trading it in when buying your 'new' used vehicle. Every dealer will want to see your 'trade', and these dealers will offer you a trade-in valuation for your vehicle, if you buy from them. There are several reasons why trading in your existing vehicle makes sense. The first one is just plain convenience. Selling a vehicle as a 'private seller' can take some effort and can be stressful. Additionally, if you buy a 'new' used vehicle for $15,000, and the dealer accepts your trade-in and gives you $3,000 for it, you will only pay HST on the difference (which in this case would be the HST on $12,000). Your trade instantly then provides you with a 'bonus' savings, equal to the HST connected to the trade value.

You can check the same web-based car search sites to get a ballpark valuation of your vehicle's worth. You can also call around to some smaller dealerships and see what they might offer you for your vehicle. You can ask your mechanic what your vehicle might be worth as a trade-in, too. All these strategies can help you get a handle on what you might be offered. Taking your vehicle to get it washed, and giving it a good interior cleaning before any dealership sees it will be time and money well spent. Having maintenance records available for inspection is wise too.

Two-vehicle family? Plan to stagger your buying

Many couples and families need two vehicles. Saddling yourselves with not one but two crushing monthly vehicle payments will obliterate your family budget. This happens again and again across the country. It stops families from saving – for retirement, for the kids' post-secondary costs, for an emergency fund – for anything!

You want to position your family to be carrying only one vehicle payment at any given time for both vehicles.

How? Intentionally staggering your quality used vehicle purchasing is the best way.

Here's how to stagger those vehicle purchases!

We know the plan when it comes to buying a quality used vehicle. We look for a vehicle – we'll call it vehicle A – coming off a four-year lease, and we keep it for six years after buying it. We trade it in once we've had it for six years (when the vehicle is ten years old). We want to have that vehicle paid off in three years. This will allow us to purchase a vehicle with our partner, for our partner's use, in the middle of that six-year period. That vehicle – we'll call it vehicle B – will be on the same 'buy a four-year-old vehicle and keep it for six years' cycle. We'll pay it off in three years too.

You'll never be making two vehicle payments in any month with this system. Here's what it looks like:

Vehicle	Year One	Year Two	Year Three	Year Four	Year Five	Year Six
A	Buy four-year-old vehicle Year one of payments	Year two of payments	Year three of payments Vehicle is paid off	No payments	No payments	No payments Sell vehicle at end of year
B				Buy four-year-old vehicle Year one of payments	Year two of payments	Year three of payments Vehicle is paid off

After this six-year cycle is over, repeat!

Remember, driving a car or truck that's almost ten years old isn't sexy, but it sure is much better than carrying crushing vehicle debt. Your future self will love you for this!

Bundle your insurance and get a better rate…and get the app!

Volume discounts work in many areas of life; insurance is definitely one of them! If you own real estate, call the insurance company that carries your home insurance policy about bringing over your auto insurance business. The savings will be significant.

Be certain to spend time discussing your auto insurance needs with your insurance agent. Auto insurance policies have standard features (such as accident benefit coverage), but you have the flexibility to both increase coverage limits and add benefits (such as accident forgiveness).

It's wise to contact an insurance broker who has access to many different insurance company offerings and can help you tailor your insurance coverage to match your needs. Insurance agents work for an insurance company, but insurance brokers work on your behalf and, as such, will shop around to present you with the most appropriate coverage at a competitive rate.

Your insurance company may offer an app that will track your driving habits. Download it and use it. It will reward you for good driving habits, such as controlling your speed and cornering safely. This will lead to lower auto insurance premiums and may also be a motivator to keep driving safely (since feedback is offered after every trip) – win/win!

Penny says...

Having snow tires on your vehicle is another win/win. Yes, they are a fantastic safety feature during the winter driving season, but alerting your auto insurance company that you have them installed on your vehicle will also lower your premiums in provinces where snow tires are not mandatory. It's a smart move!

Key takeaways from 'Mastering Your Ride'

→ understand that vehicle ownership is ridiculously expensive

→ decide whether or not you need a vehicle given the many other transportation options that are available, especially in our cities

→ understand that many of the expensive vehicles that you see on the road are simply being leased

→ realize that leasing a vehicle is not the same as owning one

→ know that vehicles depreciate in value over time and, therefore, they are certainly not investments

→ understand that dealerships want you to lease a new vehicle so doing the opposite (buying a quality used vehicle) is in your best interest

→ complete your research to identify quality used vehicles in your budget range before going to see any vehicles

→ consider purchasing vehicles that are four years old so that you will not be paying as much depreciation

→ plan on owning your vehicle for six years

→ partner with your mechanic so as to assess any vehicle before making a purchase offer

→ plan to stagger purchases (if your family needs two vehicles) so that you don't need to make multiple monthly payments

→ save for auto repair bills; they are coming

Part VI

Mastering Real Estate

In 'Mastering Real Estate', we'll look at one of life's biggest financial challenges – homeownership. The dollar amounts – and, therefore, the pressures – surrounding owning a place to call home are staggering. Low interest rates have boosted many asset classes, and this is particularly true when it comes to Canada's real estate market. Insatiable demand has been especially evident in our urban centres, where valuations have steadily climbed.

Before making an offer, a commitment to accumulate a significant down payment is needed, but further challenges – such as securing a mortgage approval and finding options in your price range – have to be faced too. The pressures create all kinds of worries and questions. Will we ever be able to afford a home? Should we wait for prices to come down before beginning our search? Will we ever pay off our mortgage? The dream of one day owning your own home can be stress-inducing.

Crucial lessons in this part of the book include understanding the factors that drive real estate prices in Canada, understanding the mortgage approval process that lenders undertake and exploring refinancing options as a homeowner when faced with significant non-mortgage debt.

The homeownership challenges can be tackled. Saving aggressively and managing expectations are important early steps. Arming yourself with knowledge around how lenders move through the mortgage application process is also important since this can give you a sense of control once you approach this hurdle. Once you are a homeowner, the responsibilities are significant. The key lessons found here will allow you to prepare yourself to face these challenges with confidence.

Real estate rocks!

There are lots of positive emotions connected with real estate ownership in our country. It makes us feel as if we have 'arrived'. We have a space to call our own – it's ours.

From a personal finance perspective, real estate tends to be a fantastic investment. Real estate that is in demand tends to go up in value over time. Gains on the sale of your principal residence (as opposed to a second property such as a cottage) are tax free. Even though it doesn't carry an acronym such as RRSP, RESP or TFSA, your investment in your principal residence is like a tax-sheltered account (in that you won't have to pay tax on your gains). For many, their home is their retirement plan, since downsizing later in life will free up cash for retirement.

Debt connected to real estate is called a mortgage. You can pay off a mortgage over a very long time period (the amortization period) such as twenty-five years, thereby using leverage (other people's money) to finance a very expensive purchase.

You are required to make a down payment. For smaller purchases, the minimum down payment can be small. For home purchases of $500,000 or less, you will need to make at least a 5% down payment. For home purchases above $500,000 but under $1 million, the down payment must be a minimum of 5% on the first $500,000, plus 10% on the dollars above that. For purchases over $1 million, the minimum is 20%.[1] Many will plan on accumulating at least a 20% down payment regardless of the purchase price so as to avoid paying mortgage default insurance.

Each mortgage payment typically has a portion that is an interest payment and a portion that is a debt repayment so, over time, you eliminate the mortgage and will own your home debt-free. Compare this to renting where each payment simply goes to the landlord to cover rent.

Penny says...

Make no mistake, renting is a viable long-term housing option. Many affordability challenges that homeowners face disappear, such as accumulating a large down payment. It goes without saying, however, that monthly rent payments are no bargain in markets where demand is high. If you go this route, you must make absolutely certain that you take steps to fund your retirement. If you don't have a workplace pension plan, this is a non-negotiable. As a renter, you won't have the option to sell your home down the road and use the proceeds as a retirement fund, so you must save aggressively and invest for growth for many years to create a retirement nest egg.

The city is where the real estate action is!

The real estate market in Canada's cities has been generally very, very strong for years. Strong urban growth along with record low interest rates have driven this. Our three largest cities – Vancouver, Toronto and Montreal – have experienced significant supply and demand imbalances in the real estate market for many years. This imbalance has made 'bidding wars' and skyrocketing prices the norm. This has spread to regions and municipalities surrounding these major centres too. Other real estate urban markets outside these regions are booming also; this is certainly a strong theme in many parts of Ontario, British Columbia and Quebec.

Location, location, location…

Location drives real estate prices. It directly impacts supply and demand. Any home or condo is worth whatever someone will pay for it. You may be shocked that a certain home in your old neighbourhood sold for X thousand dollars last month. You may feel that some sucker paid way, way too much for that home. It's a good reminder that any home or condo is worth what the markets says it is worth.

Folks want to live in urban centres. Many want to be near schools and near amenities such as shopping and entertainment districts. Many want to live in areas with green spaces, good public transit, good climate and easy access to work. Wanting to live in welcoming communities that are not only safe, but also provide a wide range of recreation and leisure options is common. Being close to parks, arenas, golf courses, ski hills, waterfronts and trails drives up real estate prices. Wanting access to quality health care is a given. In short, we want it all, and we are willing to pay for it (as seen by real estate prices in areas that offer easy access to many of these desirables).

Those areas that provide these pieces are booming – and 'location' is why.

Cottage and ski country properties are in demand!

For many, working virtually is here to stay. This has allowed workers to re-prioritize where they want to live and has pushed many to consider leaving megacities for communities that are further afar but offer great real estate value, relatively speaking. Even communities that are more than 100 kilometres outside of our megacities are seeing their local real estate markets boom. Cottage and ski country regions have also seen their real estate markets soar; living full-time in these locales has suddenly become more feasible as commuting to work becomes a thing of the past in many sectors. Demographic factors play a strong role here, too, as the number of retirees swells. Expect upward price pressures in cottage and ski country regions to continue as demand stays strong for these playground properties.

Explain how housing markets hit record highs during a global pandemic!

Who would have thought that Canada's housing market would not only hold up but would power forward during the pandemic? Canada's national housing agency (Canada Mortgage and Housing Corporation – CMHC) even got it wrong. Early on during the pandemic, the agency came out with a prediction that the country's housing market was about to plunge into a historic recession that would see the average listing price decline by 9% to 18% from pre-pandemic levels.[2] Needless to say, that caught everyone's attention.

Several months later, CMHC came forward with an admission that those predictions were considerably off the mark. Like so many other predications during the early stages of the pandemic, CMHC's forecast was just plain wrong. The reality is that those days were filled with tremendous uncertainty and trepidation; erratic forecasting became the norm in many areas. By the pandemic's second year, CMHC's view was that resale prices across the country would continue to remain strong.[3]

So, what did CMHC miss? They missed that the pandemic's damage was not equitably dolled out from a financial perspective. Yes, some sectors such as travel and tourism and 'brick and mortar' retail were hit very, very hard. However, other sectors continued to power right along. They missed that well-paid Canadians would continue to work, and that employers would be able to pivot to virtual operations with amazing speed. They missed that households would benefit from unprecedented, timely emergency government financial support. They missed that Canadians would, for the most part, do as they were told and stay home through lockdown after lockdown, causing bank balances to swell to historic levels on a national basis. They missed that interest rate cuts to record lows would make mortgages even more affordable. They missed that many young adults would turn to the Bank of Mom & Dad (which was, in many cases, now flush with cash) for help to an even greater extent when it came time to winning real estate bidding wars. They missed the waves of megacity residents who sold their properties (once they realized that working remotely wasn't going away anytime soon), converged on smaller communities within an hour's driving distance, and then bid up available real estate dramatically. Combine all that with limited supply of 'for sale' real estate in the early days of the pandemic (in some areas) along with continued strong desire to 'own', and you get a formula for skyrocketing real estate prices.

Penny says...

Time has shown that Canada's real estate market is resilient – the pandemic days certainly provided ample evidence of this. Canadians want to own real estate and there's no indication that this appetite will abate any time soon.

The real estate market has to crash, doesn't it?

In the right regions (remember 'location, location, location'), real estate has been an incredible investment for a very, very long time. In those areas, it can feel as if housing prices just move in one direction. That won't always be the case. The future will take care of that. A myriad of unknown future events – from hikes in interest rates to shifting regional employment pictures to natural disasters to you name it – will cool housing markets for periods of time even in the hottest of real estate markets.

Is the housing market going to crash? Once you look at the long-term picture and you keep in mind 'location, location, location', it doesn't seem likely that a housing market crash lasting for an extended period of time is in the cards in those locations where demand is high. In many regions, supply and demand patterns and immigration policies create a compelling counter-argument to the assertion that the housing market is doomed to experience a long-term crash.

Remember, too, that interest rate hikes often accompany economic growth. Cratering housing prices don't seem to go hand-in-hand with the increased prosperity that economic expansion brings.

Penny says...

For many regions in the country with the right mix of desirable features and characteristics, when it comes to the local real estate market, this sums it up nicely: "I wish I hadn't bought real estate in this community ten years ago!" said no one, ever!

A powerful little clue on the whereabouts of future strength in our real estate markets

As the country convulsed through the latter stages of the old, factory-based industrial era, many communities were especially hard hit. Factories closed shop forever as jobs moved overseas. Plants cut back on the number of workers. In some cases, entire industries were obliterated. Automation accelerated the job losses as machines replaced human workers in many remaining factories.

Some communities went through this violent economic shock only a few decades ago. In many cases, these communities lost their three, four or even five largest employers. These communities should have experienced economic devastation.

Yet, some of these communities are not only surviving, they are actually thriving. How is this possible?

Many of these 'survivors' have strong post-secondary institutes located in their midst. Communities with universities and colleges within their boundaries draw in bright, young minds, and many graduates decide to put down roots in those university and college towns. This entices knowledge-based companies to locate in these geographic regions to gain better access to this talent. The Toronto-Waterloo corridor is a perfect example of this. It's full of superb colleges and universities; the towns in that corridor that house post-secondary institutes are flourishing. These knowledge-based economies are prospering, and they provide some economic protection to the communities where they are located. World-class companies such as Amazon and Google aren't setting up shop in areas like Waterloo Region because they like the climate; they are picking those locations to gain access to the stream of grads coming out of schools like Conestoga College, Wilfrid Laurier University and the University of Waterloo.

Communities that are blessed to have post-secondary institutes within their boundaries might just have an edge going forward when it comes to sustained future real estate market valuations.

Penny says...

Most post-secondary students want to attend classes in person, on some level. There's no doubt that hybrid learning models (featuring a mix of both in-person and on-line course work) will continue to be offered going forward, but university and college campuses will continue to thrive. These will be magnets, attracting waves of bright, young students into those university and college towns. Many grads will decide to stay in these towns, which will be the basis for knowledge-based local economies that will continue to grow and prosper for many, many years.

Managing expectations when it comes to your real estate purchases

The average detached home prices in major Canadian markets have been on a tear for many years now. For those who are homeowners, this has been a financial bonanza. For those who are simultaneously holding investments in the stock market and watching them move ever and ever higher, the increase in household wealth has been dramatic.

For those who are on the outside of the real estate market, the feelings aren't quite the same.

When the housing market serves up bidding wars and final sale prices often land in the six-figure range above asking prices, you've got a formula for frustration. Young perspective homeowners are feeling this acutely.

The danger here is that after being outbid weekend after weekend, a young couple can easily take on more and more risk by pushing up their housing budget in a frantic attempt to 'get the next house we like'. There are significant risks involved with taking on too much debt and overpaying for a home in a supercharged real estate market.

Here's where managing expectations comes in extremely handy! Consider shifting the target to a more affordable type of property. If you were thinking about buying a small starter detached home, turn your gaze to a semi-detached home or townhouse. Apartment-style condos are even more affordable and allow you to 'get in the market'. Alternatively, consider moving away from your targeted area to the outskirts of the city, if feasible. In many regions, there are smaller communities within a reasonable drive of the city that provide much better affordability when it comes to real estate prices. The further you move away from the big city, the further your dollars will be able to stretch to buy a larger property.

Managing expectations is a big piece here. Most people in larger homes today were once renters, and likely also owned one or more smaller 'starter' properties back in the day. Realize that you are not going to buy a home like your parents' current home. Be realistic – you will lessen your chances of being disappointed with both the entire process and the outcome.

Nowadays, no one buys real estate on their own

Back in the day, it wasn't unusual to hear about someone purchasing real estate on their own. Prices were more muted and the guidelines for lending were much looser. Those days are now gone; in almost all cases, the income tests that lenders use today are just too stringent for an individual to qualify for financing on their own.

This means that you almost always need two incomes on a mortgage application to secure a mortgage in today's climate. Couples buy real estate together. Siblings buy real estate together. Moms and Dads co-sign mortgages to assist adult children with buying real estate. Friends buy real estate together.

If you are single and are looking to buy a property, it will be a challenge.

The down payment

When it comes to buying real estate, the larger the down payment, the better. As mentioned, you can buy real estate by coming up with a down payment of as low as 5% of the real estate purchase price for purchases of $500,000 or less. Many, though, will plan on coming up with at least 20% of the purchase price as a down payment. This helps to keep the mortgage payments somewhat manageable, but it also avoids the need to pay for mortgage default insurance which can add thousands to the cost of buying property. Even with a young couple both on the same page in terms of saving aggressively each pay period, it can take years to save the down payment. For a $500,000 condo in a hot market, 20% equates to $100,000. If you and your partner are starting from scratch and want to accumulate that in two years, that means that each of you needs to save almost $1,000 every biweekly pay period for the full two years. That is hard to do.

Consider living with Mom and Dad a bit longer than planned. Make a deal with Mom and Dad. The pitch would involve you being able to live rent free at home with your parents for your first year after post-secondary graduation, while you save 90% of your after-tax income. This will help you to launch, and increase the chances that you won't boomerang back. Your parents love you, but they don't want you to move out 'for good' only to come back again – and you certainly don't want to do this either.

Lenders will demand a 90-day bank statement history to confirm the source of your down payment. Keep this in mind when you are accumulating those funds. They want to ensure that the money is yours and came from legitimate sources. Part of this is due to an increased focus on anti-money laundering measures. This means that lenders often instruct their underwriters to dig, dig, dig. What they find might lead to your mortgage application being denied.

Penny says...

Is there a pattern of $500 ATM withdrawals at a local casino on your 90-day bank history? That looks like a gambling problem – MORTGAGE APPLICATION DENIED. Be especially vigilant about your financial transactions in the months leading up to your mortgage application. Securing a mortgage isn't a right – it's a privilege.

Get a mortgage pre-approval BEFORE you start real estate shopping!

Buying real estate will be one of the biggest financial events of your life and, since so much emphasis is placed on where we live, it's an emotional journey. It needs to be properly planned given the dollars involved and the emotional importance of your decision.

Having a mortgage pre-approval in hand before you ever begin house hunting is the only way to go. You will avoid the disappointment of seeing a house that you like, only to subsequently learn that you can't afford it. It will help you set a budget because the pre-approval will include the approved amount and indicate a mortgage interest rate that is usually 'held' or honoured for a period of 90 to 120 days. This doesn't lock you in, but it will provide you with an increased sense of control as you move through the buying process (since you won't be wondering about your odds of even qualifying for a mortgage).

You don't want to be in a spot where you feel 'house rich' but 'cash poor'. Mortgage affordability matters. If you take on more than you can financially handle, you will pay a heavy price for that. Your mental health will suffer. You will be constantly worrying about money.

Remember, you will have unexpected costs along the way. You will still need an emergency fund since those unexpected life events (such as a large car repair bill or a cut in hours at work) will come around at the worst possible times. If you are self-employed, be certain to have adequate insurance in place to cover you if you are unable to work.

Penny says...

Lenders might offer a pre-qualification as opposed to a pre-approval for your mortgage. The pre-qualification process involves less work in advance by the lender (in terms of confirming your income, debts, assets, etc.), and the eligible amount that you can borrow is subject to change. Be aware that any lender will thoroughly complete a due diligence process before finalizing any new mortgage.

You need a mortgage broker!

You know you need a mortgage pre-approval before you ever start shopping for any real estate. Approach a mortgage broker to accomplish this. That mortgage broker is going to have experience with clients just like you, and they will be able to match your individual circumstances with an individual lender that offers products that suit your needs. Many mortgage brokers use multiple lenders each year as they go through this match process. In addition, mortgage brokers have access to preferential interest rates given the volume of business they do with a wide host of lenders. In most cases, they will facilitate a pre-approval at no expense to you since they are compensated by the lenders when mortgages are finalized.

It's definitely worth asking any mortgage broker how many lenders they worked with during the previous calendar year. They will know this number. A large number, such as greater than 20, tells you that they actively match client needs with lender options. A low number means that they use only a small stable of lenders and may put other motivators (such as compensation from lenders) in front of your needs as a client.

The corollary of this is do not approach a Big Bank about a mortgage pre-approval. You aren't going to head in there and negotiate the best deal or get their best interest rate. You aren't going to see countless features offered to you to match your individual needs.

Penny says...

Competition is good for consumers. Use a mortgage broker and benefit from that broker's access to dozens of lenders who are competing hard for your business.

Here's the 'solution set' for mortgage applications!

Moving through the home buying process is filled with uncertainties. Since the dollar amounts and financial commitments are so large, it is a stressful process. There's more than enough stress to go around. This is certainly true for those who are doing the buying and need to be approved for a mortgage, but it is also true for the mortgage lenders too. Mortgage lenders lend money to many clients, so it makes sense that they have standardized approval processes in place to mitigate risk.

Do you remember how you loved to go up to the teacher's desk in school to check the solution set (correct answers) when you were stuck on a problem? Wouldn't it be wonderful if you were able to get a peek at any mortgage lender's approval process 'solution set'? Well, here it is! Let me introduce you to the '5 Cs of Credit'! They are collateral, credit, character, capital and capacity, and they each will be covered momentarily.

By the way, when it comes to the 5 Cs of Credit, you really can't pass the mortgage pre-approval process without scoring well on all five components. Having weakness in any one of the five components will scuttle your mortgage application. You would be wise to begin taking steps to get these financial components in a strong position well before considering a real estate purchase. It's also wise to think like a lender when it comes to the 5 Cs so as to understand the importance of each of the components.

C#1 – Collateral

Lending involves taking on risk. The most obvious and most material risk to the lender is that the client won't be able to (or will refuse to) pay back the debt. One way that lenders manage or mitigate mortgage risk is by taking steps to ensure that they have collateral for the mortgage loan. If you don't pay the lender the amounts as stipulated in the mortgage contract, they have the legal authority, as per the contract, to take control of the underlying security that is backing the mortgage, which is the real estate.

The lender, therefore, wants to make sure that the real estate is valuable and has liquidity. The lender wants to be reasonably certain that they would be able to sell the real estate to recoup their loan, if needed. Remember, to you, the mortgage is a debt or a liability, but to the lender, it's an asset. They protect the asset by ensuring that the mortgage is backed by collateral.

For this reason, lenders prefer to write mortgages for urban properties (as opposed to rural properties) since the forces of supply and demand increase the likelihood that they could liquidate or sell the real estate reasonably quickly, if needed.

Lenders may also require that a property valuation appraisal be completed. The lender's underwriter is not a field agent. The underwriter is working from home or from an office. They don't know for sure if you are overpaying for a given piece of real estate, so they will take steps to appraise the property.

There are three levels of property appraisals. The least stringent is a computerized one (Automated Valuation Model) that looks at the valuation of 'comparables', which is a term used to describe similar properties in close geographic proximity to the real estate in question (subject property). They are looking to see if your property's valuation is 'reasonable', given the recent real estate activity that has taken place near the subject property.

The next level is a 'drive-by appraisal', which is performed by an independent professional property appraiser who is impartial.

The most stringent appraisal involves an inside inspection and is referred to as 'full appraisal'. This will be the most thorough, will take the longest and will be the most expensive. The appraisal costs are normally paid by the buyer.

C#2 – Credit

We examined credit reports and credit scores in an earlier lesson, but elements of these credit risk assessment tools are worth reviewing as part of this discussion around mortgage applications. The lender will pull credit reports for all applicants listed on the mortgage application. You are going to sign a form to give permission for this. The top lenders who offer the most favourable terms don't routinely give mortgages to clients who have poor credit reports. That would be like expecting the country's top engineering schools to admit students who have low marks – it doesn't work that way.

Your credit report will include your credit score. It's the headline number; lenders look to this number first. As you would expect, if your credit report flags all kinds of problems, the credit score will be low. The opposite is also true.

The credit report is backwards looking, like your school report card. It's a 'track record' of your financial life, both the good and the bad. It's very transparent, by the way. If you were late paying that phone bill last December, it's noted. If you missed a car payment when you were on vacation earlier this year, that's there. The current balances on your credit cards are all there, too. If you applied for a credit card last year, that's captured. Every bill that you are paying on an ongoing basis, such as a utility bill or a car loan payment, is reported to the country's credit rating agencies (TransUnion and Equifax Canada) by your creditors. You gave them permission to do this when you arranged to make payments by signing a consent form.

In terms of your credit score, you are aiming to get the number to at least 680. At the very least, one of the applicants should have a score at or above that number. A top lender is going to shy away from applicants who miss that mark. Under 620 is viewed as a poor score, while 620 to 679 is seen as fair.

Penny says...

If your credit score is below 680, intentionally take steps to raise your score! Set up automated payments so that you never miss a bill payment again. Pay down your credit cards so that you are not carrying any balances from month to month. Cut back on your credit card spending so that you use up no more than 30% of your available credit card limit during any given month. Your future self will thank you for taking steps in advance of mortgage application time.

C#3 – Character

This term makes people bristle. Someone can tell you that your credit score is low and it will hurt. However, if someone tells you that your 'character' is a problem, well, to most folks, that feels like a personal attack. 'Character' in this context refers to the 'holistic you', in financial terms. What's your employment history like? How long have you lived at your current address? Carrying several debts responsibly works in your favour. For example, lenders like to see applicants with a credit report that indicates two types of debt (such as a credit card and a loan) being managed successfully over the last two or more years with a minimum $2,000 total combined credit limit. This is often referred to as '2, 2 and 2' and indicates solid evidence to a lender that you have 'credit maturity'.

You can see again that lenders are making predictions on your future reliability to make payments based on your credit maturity profile, as demonstrated by your history in this area. An applicant that presents as financially stable is more likely to have a mortgage application approved.

C#4 – Capital

On the surface, this is the easiest of the 5 Cs of Credit to understand. Capital refers to the down payment or the equity that you will bring to the table. There is a simple mathematical formula that exists at the core of the entire world of finance. It's called 'The Accounting Equation' and it looks like this:

Assets = Liabilities + Owner's Equity

You can look at a real estate purchase through this lens. The value of what you buy is on left of the equation, and the right side summarizes how you are financing the purchase (other people's money and your money).

If you are buying a $500,000 condo and have a $100,000 down payment, you will need a $400,000 mortgage. The Accounting Equation for this one asset would look like this:

- Asset = Liability + Owner's Equity

- Condo purchase price = Mortgage + Down payment

- $500,000 = $400,000 + $100,000

If you make a larger down payment for the $500,000 purchase, you would need a smaller mortgage. The opposite is also true.

The lender uses a formula called 'loan-to-value ratio' (LTV ratio) to express the size of the mortgage loan relative to the property valuation, as expressed by a percentage. For our simple example, the LTV ratio would be 80% ($400,000 / $500,000).

From the lender's perspective, mitigating risk is once again front and centre here. In our example, if you receive a $175,000 inheritance six months before buying the condo and use that extra money to boost your down payment, then you would put down $275,000 ($100,000 as originally planned + $175,000 inheritance). You would then need a smaller mortgage. The Accounting Equation for the real estate transaction would look like this:

• $500,000 condo purchase price = $225,000 mortgage + $275,000 down payment

The LTV ratio would be only 45% ($225,000 / $500,000) in this scenario.

The lower LTV ratio here with the inheritance included in the down payment (versus the prior scenario) presents an application that is now less risky from the lender's perspective.

From a risk tolerance perspective, lenders love mortgage applications with lower LTV ratios. There's less risk for them because the dollar value of the mortgage is smaller. The same advantages exist for the applicant. Accumulating a larger down payment will mean that you need a smaller mortgage; less debt is a good thing from a risk perspective. We see that at work in our example, where adding the inheritance to the planned down payment dropped the LTV ratio from 80% to only 45% while decreasing the needed mortgage from $400,000 to $225,000. The mortgage applicant is taking on less debt and, therefore, both the applicant and lender have less risk when the inheritance is included in the down payment. In our simplified example, paying off the smaller mortgage is just easier to handle for the mortgage applicant when compared to paying off the larger mortgage.

There a few LTV ratio thresholds that are important to understand.

As noted earlier, you can buy real estate by making a down payment of as little as 5% of the purchase price for homes purchased for $500,000 or less. At that level, your LTV ratio is 95% and that's as high as it can be; you have to have some of your own money in the game. Remember that the minimum down payment for home purchases above $500,000 but under $1 million will be 5% on the first $500,000 plus 10% on the amount above that level.

Accumulating a down payment of at least 20% will allow you to be eligible for what's called a 'conventional mortgage'. What if you are unable to accumulate that large of a down payment? For mortgage applications where down payments are anywhere from 5% to just under 20% (LTV ratios from just above 80% up to 95%), the mortgage is classified as a 'high ratio mortgage' or an 'insured mortgage', and the federal government will force you to purchase what is known as 'mortgage default insurance'. You are used to viewing insurance as protecting you from unexpected events. In this case, though, this insurance doesn't protect you; it protects the lender, but you will pay for it. This creates a situation that is a bit counterintuitive.

You might think that lenders would be very hesitant to lend to applicants with LTV ratios in that just above 80% up to 95% range. However, for applications with LTV ratios in that range, the applicants are forced to secure mortgage default insurance which mitigates lender risk significantly. The mortgage default insurance is available to compensate lenders for any bad debts caused by clients failing to make payments on their mortgages (which is known as defaulting). Mortgage default insurance is offered by several mortgage insurers in Canada including CMHC, our national housing agency.

Without mortgage default insurance in place, the reality is that lenders likely wouldn't approve any mortgages where applicants are only able to accumulate smaller down payments (such as 5% or 10% or 15%); there's just too much risk there. In this sense, mortgage default insurance allows Canadians to buy real estate earlier with smaller down payments. Having said that, the smaller the down payment, the larger the premium – and that premium will be added to the value of the mortgage and financed over the mortgage's life. These premiums can be large. For example, purchasing a condo for $500,000 with only a 5% down payment could see you paying nearly $20,000 in mortgage default insurance.

There are also some nuances here. For example, mortgage default insurance is only available for purchase prices below $1,000,000. Once this threshold is reached, the mortgage is considered 'uninsurable' and the minimum down payment will be 20% of the purchase price.[4]

Penny says...

For a conventional mortgage, lenders will often offer better mortgage rates to borrowers when their LTV ratio is up to 65% than, say, in the 70% to 75% range. The borrower gets rewarded for needing a smaller loan (relative to property valuation) with a lower rate.

C#5 – Capacity

Here's yet another aspect of white-hot real estate markets that is causing mortgage applicants to feel tremendous stress. Capacity refers to an applicant's ability to financially manage or handle the regular mortgage payments. Basically, if your income is such that you would have trouble covering the mortgage payments on top of your other debt payments, you won't be approved. Income verification requirements might include providing one or more of these documents: a recent pay stub, an employment letter from your employer, employment contracts or past Notice of Assessments as issued by CRA (where line 1500 – gross income – is typically used).

Lenders use formulas here to calculate the 'gross debt service' (GDS) ratio and 'total debt service' (TDS) ratio for each application. Both formulas shed light on how much of your income is 'pre-spent' each month on housing costs (using the GDS ratio) and housing costs plus other debts (using the TDS ratio). If too much of your income will be eaten up by housing costs (or housing costs plus other debts), your mortgage application will not be approved.

For those with credit scores of 680 or higher, threshold maximums for lender GDS and TDS ratios are 39% and 44% respectively. For those whose credit scores fall below that 680 level, the GDS and TDS ratio threshold maximums decrease to 35% and 42% respectively. The reality here is that lenders are simply not as willing to lend as much money to those with poorer credit scores.

Mortgage payments consist of two pieces – a repayment of the principal balance borrowed and interest on the monies borrowed. This is usually referred to as 'principal and interest'. Property owners also have to pay property taxes. For the purpose of calculating GDS and TDS, lenders also consider heating and cooling costs, which are usually estimated based on the property's square footage. The GDS ratio is calculated by taking PITH/income*100 in order to arrive at a percentage where PITH stands for mortgage principal payments, mortgage interest payments, property taxes and heating/cooling costs. The calculation is usually completed by examining monthly amounts. If you are considering a condo, half of the monthly condo fees also get added to PITH.

For a couple who both work full-time and earn a combined annual salary of $120,000 (or $10,000 monthly) with credit scores at or above 680, the maximum monthly PITH amount for a mortgage approval for a non-condo residential property would be $3,900 (39% GDS ratio). For a couple with a combined annual salary of $60,000 (or $5,000 monthly) with credit scores below 680, the maximum monthly PITH amount for a non-condo residential property would be $1,750 (35% GDS ratio).

The TDS ratio is also examined. This really is a way for the lender to get a glimpse of total debt load and the cash flow impact that debt has on the applicant each month. The TDS ratio calculation starts with PITH and then adds other monthly payments, such as credit card payments, car loan payments, student loan payments, line of credit payments, spousal or child support payments and any other debt payments. Using our earlier examples, the maximum PITH plus other monthly payments would be $4,400 (44% TDS ratio) for the $120,000 annual earners, and $2,100 (42% TDS ratio) for the $60,000 annual earners.

As you can see, in the lender's eyes, a couple earning $60,000 combined annually only has the ability to carry total debt payments of $2,100 each month. Carrying crushing monthly car payments and large monthly credit card balances will leave very little room for any kind of mortgage payment.

Penny says...

For those who are in 'business for self' (BFS), it can be tempting to aggressively write-off expenses in order to decrease income tax. You can quickly see that this severely hampers the ability to get a mortgage approval. For those with BFS income, planning several years in advance is crucial since lenders will often use a two or three-year average for BFS income to smooth out fluctuations.

As if buying real estate wasn't stressful enough, now we have a mortgage 'stress test'

The federal government saw lots of evidence of an overheated real estate market in 2016. As a result, a mortgage 'stress test' was introduced to 'test' if prospective purchasers who made down payments of less than 20% could handle potential future interest rate increases. Although it was originally introduced for only those with these insured mortgages, it has now been expanded – the continued rapid escalation in housing prices across the country made this broadening of the stress test's use inevitable.

What does the stress test mean? Federally-regulated financial institutions such as our Big Banks will now stress test your mortgage application. They want to evaluate whether you are able to afford future payments at a qualifying interest rate, which is usually much higher than the actual rate that appears in the mortgage contract with your lender. As of spring 2021, the stress test requires borrowers to prove that they could afford mortgage payments when using the higher of the 5.25% stress test rate and the negotiated mortgage contract rate plus 2%. Those with an existing mortgage will also need to pass the stress test if they apply for a HELOC, switch lenders or decide to refinance their mortgage to take advantage of lower interest rates, for example.[5]

Clearly the goal is to protect all the players involved. Given the supercharged real estate market, applying the stress test forces lenders to build in more stringent underwriting. For consumers who are pushing themselves to the edge of their affordability margins, the stress test protects them from themselves since it simulates interest rate increases. For the housing market in general, it has the potential to tamp down demand. The reality is that the federal government does not want a scenario where people can no longer afford to make their mortgage payments when mortgage renewal time arrives. Clearly, there will be consumers who won't be able to meet the stress test requirements; the stress test presents a barrier for many Canadians to enter the housing market.

Note that credit unions and other lenders that are not federally regulated are exempt from enforcing the mortgage stress test. Having said that, these lenders will certainly put your application through a strenuous review to examine affordability.

Penny says...

Almost 60% of polled millennial Canadians believe that it's a good time to buy real estate in order to take advantage of today's low interest rates.[6] Additional government housing restrictions are certainly a possibility if white-hot demand creates drastic imbalances in the housing market.

Bruised credit? There are options

Life happens. Some events can negatively impact our financial profile. Unexpectedly losing a job or a massive shock like a global financial crisis can have ripple effects that careen across every element of our financial life. For some, making minimum payments on credit cards might be the only way to make ends meet. Defaulting (stopping debt repayments) might be a reality for others. A major illness or a divorce can turn your world upside down on every level, and your finances invariably take a hit.

Hopefully, you are able to get back on your feet financially. Unfortunately, your credit score will likely have been hurt. A mortgage applicant who moved through even a two or three-month financial struggle last year, where they missed several months of bill payments due to a life crisis, will have a credit report that captures that, and a credit score that will be negatively impacted by that for years. Generally speaking, negative information will stay on your credit report for six years. A bankruptcy and late payments are examples of the kind of negative information that lingers on your credit report many years after the fact.

Obviously, there are mortgage applicants who have this kind of bruised credit history. Traditional lenders such as the Big Banks (referred to as 'A' lenders) will turn down new mortgage applicants with bruised credit. The story doesn't end there, though. Those with bruised credit can access a wide range of alternative lenders ('B' lenders and 'C' lenders) by using the mortgage broker channel.

Not surprisingly, those needing to turn to alternative lenders will pay a much higher interest rate for a mortgage given the increased risk that those lenders assume. Some 'B' lenders will also have a limited offering of mortgage options. It's also worth noting that alternative lenders in the 'C' lending space often mitigate risk by having a focus on what's called 'equity lending', which means that their attention is on the house (urban properties are preferred) when it comes to their internal underwriting standards. This means that there is limited (or no) focus on income tests. The typical length of the mortgage will be very short (one-year term) meaning that this is not a long-term solution for borrowers. From a borrower's perspective, the plan often involves turning to the alternative lenders as a short-term solution to buy time while taking steps to 'clean up the credit profile' (in an attempt to get back to the 'A' space when the mortgage renews in one year). Be warned, though – this involves large fees for borrowers. This is a strong motivator to get the credit profile cleaned up so as to successfully apply to an 'A' lender in 12 months.

Use a trusted professional realtor to guide you through purchasing real estate

When it comes to buying residential real estate, buyers don't pay realtor fees; this bill is picked up by the seller. As the buyer, you won't need to pay for professional realtor advice, so plan on having a realtor by your side as you move through the process of buying real estate.

Professional realtors have access to up-to-the minute market data, which will help you to set expectations, and go into the process with a plan. They have their fingers on the pulse of a local real estate market, and will see patterns and trends that aren't always obvious to inexperienced buyers. Be sure to ask friends and associates for referrals, and check a realtor's references. Having confidence in your realtor is invaluable. Be assured that they will be motivated to help you purchase a property since realtors don't get paid unless that purchase happens. In hot markets that are moving fast, where multiple bids over the asking price are the norm and the chances of being 'outbid' on properties you like each weekend are high, a professional realtor's guidance and perspective will prove to be invaluable on many, many levels.

When it comes to selling property, as mentioned, you will be responsible for paying the realtor commission to the buyer's real estate agent and your realtor too. Expect to pay in the neighbourhood of 5% of the selling price for realtor fees (2.5% to both realtors). You can choose to go with a realtor who will discount their fees on the sell side; you will still need to pay the buyer's realtor a commission. You can also choose to use a fixed-fee real estate service that will support you through the process at a fraction of the full-service cost. Using this route, the realtor commission savings can easily add up to tens of thousands of dollars.

Penny says...

There are many layers of fees and expenses to consider when buying real estate. Yes, the buyer is spared the costs of paying realtor fees, but closing costs such as legal fees, title searches, land transfer charges and moving costs all are a reality. Your realtor and mortgage agent can help you get a sense of these costs as the time approaches, but go in knowing that there are significant costs involved with such a large transaction.

Buying real estate – conditionally!

There are obvious factors to consider when putting in an offer to buy real estate, such as the offer amount and closing date. Generally speaking, you want to be sure that any offer you make also includes conditions. Two crucial ones are a financing condition and a home inspection condition. These will be time-sensitive: typically, they will expire five business days after an offer is accepted, so you will need to move quickly. The benefit to including these conditions in the offer is pretty straightforward; your offer to buy is 'contingent' on these conditions being satisfied. If the financing condition or home inspection condition aren't satisfied, you can back out of the deal with no penalty. There will be pressure here; a professional realtor will guide you through these stressful days.

The financing condition allows you, as the buyer, to now go back to your mortgage lender with details about the actual property that you have purchased conditionally. The lender can then quickly move through the underwriting process with renewed visibility on pieces such as the actual property itself.

Your mortgage pre-approval will hopefully then become an approved mortgage if this underwriting goes smoothly. You have the option of turning to a different lender for the actual mortgage approval too; arranging a pre-approval doesn't commit you to dealing with that specific lender. Your mortgage broker may be able to find another lender who has a better mortgage product available given your circumstances. You have maximum flexibility here if you are working with a mortgage broker. Remember, too, that lenders can check your credit report prior to closing to ensure that your credit profile hasn't materially deteriorated, so be intentional about taking steps to maintain your good credit score.

A home inspection condition allows you to inspect the property. You will want to hire a professional home inspector to get inside the home; a full, written report will capture the findings. That crack in the basement that you saw during the open house? The home inspector can tell you whether or not it is a worry. Wondering if you need to replace the roof or the air conditioner in the near future? The home inspector's report will provide those details. If, for example, the home inspection report identifies a major, undisclosed flaw in the home's structure, you can consult with your realtor and real estate lawyer about options going forward. Those options might include resolving the repair issues with the seller before the closing date or walking away from the offer, and getting your deposit back.[7]

Penny says...

In hot markets, sellers are in control. Buyers may feel pressure to put in an offer with no conditions, which is often called 'going in firm'. Be extremely cautious here since including conditions (such as a financing condition and a home inspection condition) provides invaluable protection for you as a buyer!

Maintaining real estate doesn't rock

Your home is a major investment, and it will likely go up in value over the years. You need to take steps to maintain it in order to protect value. Some of those steps are inexpensive (such as changing furnace filters), while others (like a bathroom renovation) represent major expenditures.

You should be intentionally budgeting for big ticket repair and maintenance costs connected with homeownership. Plan on needing to spend approximately 1% of your home's market value each year on these costs. This won't be linear. Some years, you might not need to spend much at all. Don't let this good fortune lull you into cutting back on saving for these costs, especially if you are in an older home. The costs associated with needed repairs and maintenance can deliver body blows to your finances. Examples of needed work can include replacing windows, doors, the roof, the driveway, the deck, flooring, counter tops, toilets, sinks, major appliances, bathroom vanities, steps and stairway repairs. In an older home, this is the reality. Expensive renovations are often a reality, too. These can be disruptive and stressful since they often involve lining up tradespeople who are extremely busy, and have many projects on the go simultaneously. Even a new home likely won't come with a deck, fencing nor a paved driveway as of the closing date, let alone a finished basement. Save for these costs – they are coming – and realize that you need to maintain your property, even if the reality is that the money spent often does not translate into immediate dollar for dollar increases in market value.

When it comes to condos, the monthly fees can be expensive. However, they all but eliminate the nasty repair and maintenance bill surprises that many homeowners experience. Condo fees are predictable, and the headaches involved with arranging to have the work done are handled by someone else. Speak to a homeowner who is spending $25,000 to $30,000 to replace windows and doors in an older home and you will feel their pain. Condo owners don't experience these shocks.

Penny says...

Canadians love their homes, and taking on home renovation projects is common. For example, during the pandemic, a majority of those polled expected to undertake a renovation at home in the next two years; backyard projects along with bathroom and kitchen work were all top priorities.[8] Be intentional about saving on a regular basis for home upkeep costs. They are coming, they can add up quickly, and they are needed when it comes to protecting your largest investment.

Property taxes are taxing!

You will pay property taxes when you own real estate. These taxes are set by municipal governments and school boards; they help to pay for local services such as policing, fire fighting, libraries and roads. Note that property taxes are calculated using the 'assessed value' for the individual property. When market prices are aggressively rising, this assessed value will badly lag the market value of the property. This will lead to further increases in property tax bills as the stated valuation moves up in increments annually in an effort to catch up to the actual market price.

A very rough estimate for the property tax amount is 1% of the assessed value, but you will be able to see the current property tax amount on the listing for any property that is for sale. The more a property is worth, the higher the property tax bill. You won't get any better service for this extra tax, though; you will pay more simply because your property is worth more.

Amortization periods and mortgage duration or term

Small loans can be paid back quickly. The opposite is true for large loans. Mortgages are just that – large loans. Whereas car loan payments might be stretched out or 'amortized' over five years, a mortgage will be amortized over a much longer period of time (typically 25 years) so that the payments are manageable. If lenders required you to pay off the mortgage balance in three years, who would be able to afford a mortgage? Also of note is that 30-year mortgages are available from some lenders. Moving to a 30-year mortgage is a way to decrease regular payments, but this will increase the overall dollars paid since the loan is stretched out over a longer period. In addition, you will need to come up with at least 20% as a down payment since mortgages with amortization periods of longer than 25 years are not eligible for mortgage default insurance.

Although your lender will amortize mortgage payments over many decades, your particular mortgage contract will have a set term or length. This protects both the lender and the mortgage applicant since many factors in the economy can change over time, and contracts that lock both sides in for too many years involve taking on too much uncertainty. As a result, typical mortgage terms last from one to 10 years, with five-year terms being common.

Closed versus open mortgages

Both closed mortgages and open mortgages have payment schedules. Open mortgages, however, allow the borrower to pay off more of the balance at any time during the mortgage term with no penalty, whereas closed mortgages don't offer that feature. Having said that, many fully-featured closed mortgages will have clauses that allow borrowers to make additional payments during the term of the mortgage.

Fixed-rate mortgages versus variable-rate mortgages

The interest rates attached to variable-rate (or adjustable-rate) mortgages are driven by short-term interest rates. In Canada, short-term rates are set by our central bank, the Bank of Canada. The key Canadian government rate is the policy interest rate as set by the Bank of Canada, which is also known as the Bank of Canada's target for the overnight rate. The Bank of Canada sets or moves this rate from time to time as a way to stimulate or slow down the county's economy, depending on the circumstances. The Big Banks and other financial institutions use this Bank of Canada rate to set what's called their 'prime rate' or the 'prime lending rate'. All loan interest rates are set based on 'prime'.

Central banks around the world, including the very powerful and influential US Federal Reserve System (affectionately called 'the Fed'), use short-term rates to control inflation. High inflation isn't good because it spirals out of control and can ruin an economy. If prices are rising at 10% per year, you will want a pay package that increases by greater than 10% a year, which causes prices to keep rising. That's not good. If prices are falling, that's called deflation. If car prices keep dropping, everyone delays buying cars and, consumers top spending – not good. So, central banks want inflation to fall in a range – usually in the 1% to 3% range – and they take actions that impact interest rates to 'help' inflation stay in that range. Dropping rates is like pushing down the gas pedal on the economy – it's designed to accelerate the economy since it makes spending and taking on debt less burdensome. Raising rates does the opposite. During both the 2008-2009 financial crisis and the pandemic, for example, central banks around the globe pushed short-term interest rates down to extremely low levels in an effort to support economies, and spur on both consumer spending and business investment.

Fixed-rate mortgage rates, on the other hand, are driven by long-term interest rates. The long-term rates are set by the bond market. Stocks trade on the stock market. Bonds (which are a debt instrument used by governments and corporations to raise money for many purposes) trade on the bond market. Normally, bond investors expect a higher interest rate when they tie up their money for longer periods of time. This creates what's known as the yield curve. Yield just refers to the interest rate that corresponds to a given debt instrument. In normal times, the yield curve rises as you move out into longer timeframes such as 5, 10 and 30 years. In times of economic uncertainty, the yield curve can invert; investors will accept lower interest rates because they predict that the prospects for long-term growth are very weak. This is often a harbinger for a recession, which is a term describing the overall economy when it is shrinking or contracting – not good.

Canadians love their five-year fixed-rate Big Bank mortgages – and so do the Big Banks!

There are good reasons why you would choose a five-year fixed-rate mortgage. The main one centres around certainty. You know your payments for the next five years. You know your mortgage's interest rate for the next five years. If interest rates move up tomorrow or next month, your mortgage's interest rate won't go up because your rate is 'fixed'. It appears in your mortgage contract. It gives you peace of mind for 60 wonderful months.

Compare this to selecting a variable-rate mortgage. If you go with a variable-rate mortgage and short-term interest rates move up in the economy, the interest rate on your mortgage will go up, too. Your mortgage payments will automatically rise. The opposite happens if interest rates move down. Those who are risk averse don't like this uncertainty despite the fact that variable-rate mortgages often have attached interest rates that are lower than fixed rates for the same mortgage term.

Make no mistake, you pay for this peace of mind when you take the five-year fixed-rate mortgage at your neighbourhood Big Bank. You will pay a premium for this; as noted, fixed rates are almost always higher than variable rates when it comes to mortgages. Big Banks need to be compensated for locking their money up for five years. Recall that your mortgage is actually an asset to the Big Banks, and those bankers set mortgage rates so as to make money on mortgage business.

One of the largest sources of income for Big Banks is called 'net interest income' and it's basically the difference between what's charged on loans and debts, less what is paid in interest on deposits. Our deposits get pushed out the back door by our Big Banks as car loans and mortgages. Obviously, the more dollars the Big Banks push out the door in the form of loans, the more money they make. If you have ever had a Big Bank customer service representative (CSR) ask you about getting a credit card or a US dollar savings account or a chequing account, that CSR is simply doing what they are told; they are selling products. They are trying to reach branch goals by selling you another product. Each product further tethers you as a customer. View five-year Big Bank mortgages this way; they want to keep your business, and having you make payments over the next five years is a great way to increase the likelihood that you will keep your bank account and perhaps also get a credit card and a car loan with that same bank. All these products generate ongoing, predictable revenue for the Big Banks.

One other key reason why Big Banks love five-year fixed-rate mortgages is that they come with massive penalties (often tens of thousands of dollars) that kick in if and when the mortgage contract is broken. These penalties can often 'monopolize' you as a client because breaking out of the mortgage contract is so expensive that you just ride out the 60 months.

Why would anyone possibly break their mortgage contract given these massive Big Bank penalties? There are reasons for this. Examples include unexpectedly needing or choosing to move before the five-year term expires or deciding to take advantage of dropping interest rates that may become available in the marketplace. You may be surprised to learn that many Canadians don't make it to the end of their five-year mortgage terms. Big Banks reap the benefits of this since they typically calculate the penalty for breaking the mortgage contract by charging the greater of three months' interest or the interest rate differential (IRD). Ever wonder why your Big Bank's posted mortgage rates are often so high? Yes, this gives them ample room to drop the interest rate if you request this during the negotiation. Another reason is that the IRD calculation is a big moneymaker for them since they normally use the inflated 'posted rate' in the number crunch that's used to arrive at the penalty for breaking the mortgage contract. Monoline lenders that can be accessed through the mortgage broker channel normally use rates that are aggressively discounted, so the IRD isn't as punishing.

The best mortgage is the one that you just paid off! Accelerate those payments!

What seems like an irrelevant decision (frequency of mortgage payments) when you finalize your mortgage contract actually matters significantly. Accelerate your payments by making them on a weekly basis if offered, as opposed to stretching payments out to a monthly timeframe. The math helps you here, since payment dollars go towards your mortgage principal each week (as opposed to only once a month, for example).

Deep within a fully-featured closed mortgage contract, you'll find additional crucial clauses called prepayment privileges that allow you to pay off your mortgage more quickly. Ask about these features well before you sign the mortgage contract. Examples include clauses that permit you to increase the amount of your payments or make lump sum payments. Those extra dollars will go directly towards the mortgage's principal, and decrease the overall dollars that you will spend over time (since the debt is being paid off in an accelerated fashion). Commit to taking advantage of these clauses as you make your way through the mortgage's life. They can literally allow you to pay off your mortgage many years earlier than expected. Remember, the best mortgage is the one you just finished paying off!

Penny says...

You've just received a pay raise - congratulations! How do you decide which debt to pay down? Or should you invest? When it comes to choices such as these, the interest rate associated with each debt is important to consider. For example, paying off a credit card balance on a card with a 29.99% annual interest rate creates a 29.99% return, whereas putting that extra savings on a 2.99% mortgage will not give you the same benefit. When it comes to investing and if you are a parent, don't forget that you will get a 20% return via the CESG for a deposit into an RESP (within limits). Weigh these considerations when deploying surplus savings dollars.

I am a homeowner, but I have lots of non-mortgage debt – like credit card balances and car loans. Time to consider refinancing!

We looked at debt consolidation earlier but it's worth revisiting here. After years of making mortgage payments and with rising real estate markets, many homeowners realize that they have built up a significant amount of equity in their homes. Carrying lots of non-mortgage debt, such as large credit car balances and multiple car loans, creates an opportunity for homeowners to consolidate those other debts by using their home equity. This involves paying off your existing mortgage (along with all those non-mortgage debts), and replacing it with a new one. This is called refinancing, and it's a great way to decrease the interest rate on those non-mortgage debts in a significant way. A home equity line of credit might or might not be a better option too. A mortgage broker can explore options and examine the advantages (saved interest costs) and disadvantages (fees for breaking out of an existing mortgage with the refinancing option) as part of a refinancing conversation.

We're first-time homebuyers – HELP!

The federal government recognizes that getting into a hot housing market is a challenge. There is a 'First-time Home Buyer Incentive' that basically involves the federal government standing alongside you as you purchase your first residential property. With this program, the government will actually benefit with you if your home price rises over time; the opposite is also true.

The program is structured such that you can borrow 5% or 10% of the purchase price of the residential property, knowing that you must pay back the same percentage of the home's value at the time of sale (or before 25 years elapses if you still own the property). There are many rules and restrictions, but the net benefit is that the federal government is putting up some money at the time of purchase. This will have the effect of decreasing the size of your mortgage, and thus deceasing your mortgage payments. Remember, though, that the federal government is your partner here, and you will likely need to pay them back more than they originally gave you. For example, if you receive a 5% incentive on a modest $200,000 purchase, that equates to a $10,000 incentive. If you later sell for $300,000, that will entail repaying 5% of that amount or $15,000.[9] This would cause most to wonder about the wisdom of using this program since real estate prices do tend to rise over the long term. It will come as no surprise that this program has had very little take-up.[10]

There is a federal Home Buyers' Plan (HBP) which is also designed to help first-time home buyers. This plan allows you to withdraw money from your RRSP for a qualifying home. The funds must be paid back within a 15-year window, and you are able to withdraw up to $35,000. Thankfully, this plan has no 'government equity stake' component. It's structured such that you can withdraw the funds without having the RRSP issuer withhold tax on the withdrawn dollars. By participating in this plan, you forego the tax-free growth potential of those dollars while they're inside an RRSP, but, again, there is no worry about paying back any amount beyond the withdrawn sum, as long as repayment timeframes are honoured.[11]

Rental income properties are investments

In urban markets, there is often a very active market for rental income properties. Young professionals often like to live downtown, which creates significant demand for condos. Investors scoop up these condos, purchasing them as rentals. The business model is easy to understand. It involves having the rent that the condo tenants pay each month cover both the mortgage and condo fee payments. At some point down the road as retirement approaches, the owner can then sell the property, pay off the remaining mortgage and use the after-tax profits as a retirement fund. As long as the asset value rises (as real estate markets in urban centres are prone to do over the long term), this is a solid investment model.

Note that you need to consider 'after-tax profits' here. Remember that selling a primary residence generates no capital gains. If you sell your primary home for $750,000 and bought it a decade ago for $550,000, that $200,000 capital gain is tax free. This is one of the reasons why homeownership is such a good investment over the long term. However, a homeowner who buys an investment property needs to be instantly aware that the capital gain generated on the investment property will be taxable. It's fair to say that owning an investment property is like having a business; however, the CRA treats the rental cash flow as rental income as opposed to business income. As a result, the CRA allows you to expense costs related to the rental income. This means that you are able to deduct costs such as utilities, maintenance, property tax, advertising and interest expenses. Given the dollar amounts involved, accurately tracking allowable expenses along with consulting a tax professional are non-negotiables for any rental income property owner.

Key takeaways from 'Mastering Real Estate'

→ understand that 'location, location, location' continues to drive real estate valuations

→ know that the demand for urban real estate has been high in this country

→ realize that any knowledge-based community (with a strong post-secondary institute presence) is well-positioned for future growth

→ keep in mind that it is now very difficult for an individual to secure a mortgage approval without someone else on the application

→ understand the '5 Cs of Credit' to prepare for the mortgage approval process

→ use the services of a mortgage broker

→ save for ongoing upkeep costs as a homeowner since they are coming

→ understand that there are significant differences between fixed-rate mortgages and variable-rate mortgages

→ accelerate your mortgage payments

→ consider refinancing options as a homeowner when carrying significant non-mortgage debt

→ know that government programs exist to assist first-time homebuyers

→ realize that rental income properties are an investment option

Conclusion

The final lesson I want to share with you is really like so many other lessons in this book. It's simple, but not easy. It's not a hot stock tip, nor a 'get rich quick' idea. I hope that after seeing it, you will instantly say to yourself "I should have expected that!"

The final lesson is "Seize the day – action what you have learned from reading this book!"

Your personal financial life is serious, serious business that directly impacts you each and every single day. The lessons in this book require patience (there were no 'get rich quick' schemes) and self-discipline. Remember, though, that your life is FINITE, and no one should care more about your money than you. I like to think of UPC – live your life with Urgency, Passion and Compassion!

If you struggle with actioning a particular lesson, write down a goal, and be sure to align your actions and thoughts to achieve that goal. Use the SMART goal format, if needed. Making sure that your goal statements are specific, manageable, attainable, relevant and time-bound will help. Be sure, too, to tell others about your goal; that will increase your commitment level!

You want to follow these steps repeatedly so as to create a pattern of financial success – and then repeat again. This will build confidence, and increase your commitment level. Remember – KISS – keep it simple... seriously! Your future self will thank you! The payback is that following these lessons will allow you to thrive, not just survive, financially. You will take control of your money as opposed to letting money worries control you. You will be in a position to prosper financially, spending much less time worrying about money while, at the same time, being able to seek out ways to give back to make the world a better place!

Use positive self-talk relentlessly. You can do this. Hopefully, Penny has helped show you the way!

Post-Conclusion

There's a stunning lack of significant personal financial literacy content being taught in this country, and around the planet. As noted earlier, the Organisation for Economic Co-operation and Development (OECD) has stated that this is harmful on many, many levels.

The OECD also notes that "Supporting financial education can be viewed by the main public, private and civil stakeholders as a critical long-term investment in human capital."[1]

I couldn't agree more.

Therefore, I'm calling for a three-step approach to address this now since *education* (and not government bailouts targeted at consumers and/or businesses) is the only way forward. Here are the three steps:

1. Make it a requirement that each secondary school student in the country successfully completes at least one personal finance course in order to graduate. There are many secondary school courses (such as marketing and accounting) that contain financial literacy content, but they are often labelled as 'electives', so not all students complete them. An age-specific, mandatory course in personal finance during the secondary school years would be an excellent way for all students to learn key personal finance content. This course would build on the financial literacy content found in elementary school curriculum.

2. Make it a requirement that every secondary school math course in the country contains financial literacy content that's embedded in at least one curriculum strand. Wouldn't it be wonderful if math courses were more practical!

3. Make it a requirement that at least one course in personal financial literacy be successfully completed in order to graduate from any college diploma program, apprenticeship certification program or university degree

program. This kind of mandatory, dedicated financial literacy education would be invaluable to students during their post-secondary years on countless levels. Surprisingly, many of our country's university business schools don't teach much personal finance content, so significant strides are possible right across the entire post-secondary world in Canada.

Delivering financial literacy education using these steps would put Canadians in a position to take control of their financial lives. This can no longer be a hit-and-miss proposition; it must be viewed as an attainable goal for all of us. We have a moral imperative to put all Canadians in a position to thrive financially, and mandatory personal financial literacy education is the foundation for reaching this goal.

Endnotes

Introduction

1. FP Canada "Financial Stress" Survey, May 2020

2. "Canadian Payroll Association's 12th Annual Survey of Working Canadians", September 2020

3. "Financial Education in Schools", International Network on Financial Education, Organisation for Economic Co-operation and Development, 2012, https://www.oecd.org/finance/financial-education/FinEdSchool_web.pdf

4. Canadian Foundation for Economic Education, "Youth Survey: Learning About Money", November 16, 2018

5. "Financial Education in Schools", International Network on Financial Education, Organisation for Economic Co-operation and Development, 2012, https://www.oecd.org/finance/financial-education/FinEdSchool_web.pdf

6. "Financial Education in Schools", International Network on Financial Education, Organisation for Economic Co-operation and Development, 2012, https://www.oecd.org/finance/financial-education/FinEdSchool_web.pdf

7. "Financial Education in Schools", International Network on Financial Education, Organisation for Economic Co-operation and Development, 2012, https://www.oecd.org/finance/financial-education/FinEdSchool_web.pdf

Part I – Mastering the Money Mindset

1. MNP Consumer Debt Index, January 2021, FP Canada "Cross Country Checkup", November 2020

2. CIBC Poll, "Am I saving enough to retire? Vast majority of Canadians just don't know", February 8, 2018

3. Financial Planning Standards Council "Financial Stress" Survey, May 2018

4. "Why Do People Divorce?", Ann Gold Buscho Ph.D., Psychology Today website, posted February 22, 2020, https://www.psychologytoday.com/ca/blog/better-divorce/202002/why-do-people-divorce

5. Canadian Payroll Association 2018 Survey of Employed Canadians, September 2018

6. Ipsos Financial Service Excellence Awards

7. FP Canada "2020 Financial Stress Index", July 2020

8. https://www.playsmart.ca/lottery-instant-games/lottery/odds/

Part II – Mastering Debt

1. https://www.canada.ca/en/financial-consumer-agency/services/credit-reports-score/information-credit-report.html

2. https://www.canada.ca/en/financial-consumer-agency/services/credit-reports-score/credit-report-score-basics.html

3. CMHC Report – "Home Equity Lines of Credit Use in Canada" – September 25, 2018

4. Financial Consumer Agency of Canada Report – "Home Equity Lines of Credit – Consumer Knowledge and Behaviour" Report – January 15, 2019

5. Hoyes, Michalos & Associates Bankruptcy Study as reported in The Waterloo Region Record, page A1, September 7, 2018

Part III – Mastering Investing

1. www.cdic.ca

2. https://www.cudicbc.ca/index.aspx?p=cudic/index

3. https://www.fsrao.ca/consumers/credit-unions-and-deposit-insurance

4. https://www.spglobal.com/spdji/en/indices/equity/sp-tsx-composite-index/#overview

5. https://www.spglobal.com/spdji/en/indices/equity/sp-500/#overview

6. Berkshire Hathaway Inc., 2020 Annual Report, page 2

7. Norman Rothery, The Globe and Mail 'Globe Investor', "If you want peace of mind as an investor, play the long game", page B8, October 6, 2020

8. Ruth Saldanha, "Canadian investors get a 'Below Average' fee experience", Morningstar.ca, September 17, 2019

9. S&P Indices vs. Active (SPIVA) Canada Mid-Year 2020, October 13, 2020, https://www.spglobal.com/spdji/en/spiva/article/spiva-canada-mid-year-2020

10. S&P Indices vs. Active (SPIVA) Canada Year-End 2020 Report, March 18, 2021, https://www.spglobal.com/spdji/en/spiva/article/spiva-canada/

11. S&P Indices vs. Active (SPIVA) U.S. Year-End 2020 Report, March 11, 2021, https://www.spglobal.com/spdji/en/spiva/article/spiva-us

12. Organisation for Economic Co-operation and Development (2021), Long-term interest rates (indicator). doi: 10.1787/662d712c-en (accessed on June 15, 2021)

13. Berkshire Hathaway Inc., 2020 Annual Report, page 5

14. Thomas Franck, "Here's a list of stock bull markets through time and how this new one stacks up", CNBC.com, August 18, 2020, https://www.cnbc.com/2020/08/18/heres-a-list-of-stock-bull-markets-through-time-and-how-this-new-one-stacks-up.html

15. Matt Phillips, "This market is nuts!", The New York Times, August 18, 2020

16. https://dqydj.com/sp-500-return-calculator/

17. http://www.econ.yale.edu/~shiller/data.htm

18. Berkshire Hathaway Inc., 2019 Annual Report, page 11

19. https://www.vanguard.ca/en/investor/home

20. https://www.blackrock.com/ca/investors/en/products/product-list

21. "The portfolio currency-hedging decision, by objective and block by block", Vanguard Research, Daren R. Roberts; Paul M. Bosse, CFA; Scott J. Donaldson, CFA, CFP ®; Matthew C. Tufano, August 2018   vanguardcanada.ca,   https://www.vanguardcanada.ca/documents/portfolio-currency-hedging-decision.pdf

22. John C. Bogle, "The Little Book of Common Sense Investing", 2007, pages 78 and 86

23. Rob Carrick, The Globe and Mail 'Globe Investor', "'Recoveries never go in a straight line'", page B8, July 4, 2020

24. Charles Schwab report entitled "The Schwab Self-Directed Brokerage Account Indicators" for the quarter ending June 30, 2020

Part IV – Mastering Your RRSP, RESP & TFSA

1. Fraser Institute, "Tax Freedom Day: 2020 Report", May 19, 2020

2. Fraser Institute, "Fraser Research Bulletin", May 2021

3. BDO Canada Ltd. website, 2018 BDO Canada Affordability Index Report

4. Government of Canada website – CPP retirement pension: Overview

5. Government of Canada website – Registered Retirement Income Fund (RRIF)

6. https://www.canada.ca/en/revenue-agency/services/tax/individuals/topics/rrsps-related-plans/what-home-buyers-plan/participate-home-buyers-plan.html

7. https://www.canada.ca/en/revenue-agency/services/tax/individuals/topics/rrsps-related-plans/lifelong-learning-plan.html

8. https://www150.statcan.gc.ca/n1/daily-quotidien/200813/dq200813b-eng.htm

9. https://www150.statcan.gc.ca/n1/daily-quotidien/200813/dq200813b-eng.htm

10. Malcolm Hamilton and Philip Cross, "Risk and Reward in Public Sector Pension Plans: A Taxpayer's Perspective", Fraser Institute, 2018

11. https://www.canada.ca/en/department-finance/news/2021/04/budget-2021-a-canada-wide-early-learning-and-child-care-plan.html

12. FP Canada, "Housing Affordability Survey", Survey by Leger, April 2019

13. Government of Canada website – Choosing the right Registered Education Savings Plan (RESP)

14. Government of Canada website – Registered Education Savings Plans (RESPs)

15. https://www.wealthsimple.com/en-ca/product/invest

16. Government of Canada website – Using your RESP, https://www.canada.ca/en/services/benefits/education/education-savings/resp/use.html#h2

Part V – Mastering Your Ride

1. Deloitte.Insights, "Electric Vehicles – Setting a course for 2030", Deloitte's Global Automotive Team, July 28, 2020, https://www2.deloitte.com/us/en/insights/focus/future-of-mobility/electric-vehicle-trends-2030.html

2. https://www.autotrader.ca/

Part VI – Mastering Real Estate

1. https://www.canada.ca/en/financial-consumer-agency/services/mortgages/down-payment.html

2. CMHC, "2020 Housing Market Outlook" – Special Edition, May 27, 2020

3. CMHC, "Housing Market Outlook", Spring 2021

4. https://www.canada.ca/en/financial-consumer-agency/services/ mortgages/down-payment.html

5. https://www.canada.ca/en/financial-consumer-agency/services/ mortgages/preparing-mortgage.html

6. 2021 Scotiabank Housing Poll, April 12, 2021, Scotiabank.com website

7. https://www.reco.on.ca/ask-joe-question/offer-buy-home-accepted-home-inspection-found-major-issue-options/

8. 2021 Scotiabank Housing Poll, April 12, 2021, Scotiabank.com website

9. Government of Canada website, https://www.placetocallhome.ca/fthbi/ first-time-homebuyer-incentive

10. Robyn Urback, "Not included in the budget: real help to cool runaway real estate markets", The Globe and Mail, page A7, April 20, 2021

11. https://www.canada.ca/en/revenue-agency/services/tax/individuals/ topics/rrsps-related-plans/what-home-buyers-plan/participate-home-buyers-plan.html

Post-Conclusion

1. "Financial Education in Schools", International Network on Financial Education, Organisation for Economic Co-operation and Development, 2012, https://www.oecd.org/finance/financial-education/FinEdSchool_web.pdf

Meet Mr. Masters

Fred Masters is the President & Founder of Masters Money Management. He is a financial literacy expert with three decades of experience as a professional educator in Ontario delivering senior finance courses. He has an absolute passion for teaching others about personal finance.

Mr. Masters founded Masters Money Management in 2018, and has given personal financial literacy presentations to a wide variety of audiences including university students, both elementary and secondary school students, parent groups and during business 'lunch & learn' sessions. He is a sought-after media commentator on financial literacy in schools, having appeared in articles in The Globe and Mail and The Waterloo Region Record, along with making multiple radio appearances. He is a licensed mortgage agent, and is part of the Mortgage InGenuity Inc. team based out of Kitchener, Ontario.

He lives in Waterloo Region with his wife, Kathy Doherty-Masters, a retired professional educator and former Healthy Active Living Consultant. The couple love to travel – Mr. Masters writes for www.whattravelwriterssay. com – and they are avid Olympic fans, having attended over 30 events at four Olympic Games (Athens, Beijing, Vancouver and London). Their sons, Andrew and Brendan, are former university student-athletes, who have now transitioned to professional life. Andrew is a professional hockey goaltender and Brendan is a professional educator.

Follow @MastersMoney101 and visit
www.mastersmoneymanagement.ca for further details.